I AM A SENSATION

Gerry Goldberg   George Wright

McClelland and Stewart Limited

TABLE OF CONTENTS

BEULAH 3
poems of innocence, childhood, idiocy

WHAT DREAMS TELL 13
poems of dreams, fantasies, duties to oneself and to the world

HOMO VIATOR 27
poems about man and God, the quest, the supernatural, and journeying

THE DARKNESS OF BEASTS 41
poems about man, animals, nature, missing links, and education

BY THE YEAR 2000: EUTHANASIA 55
poems about growing old, the contemplation of death, and memory

THERE ARE MORE THINGS IN HEAVEN AND EARTH, HORATIO, THAN ARE DREAMT OF IN YOUR PHILOSOPHY 65
poems of philosophy, speculation, and mysticism

THERE IS CONSIDERABLE EVIDENCE THAT LEARNING IS PRIMARILY A SENSORY AND EMOTIONAL EXPERIENCE 79
poems of learning, education, discourse, and man's failure to see, feel, and hear

THERE OUGHT TO BE A LAW SO A MAN KNOWS WHETHER HE'S DOING RIGHT OR WRONG 93
poems of warfare, violent death, fear, and man's inner search

OUT OF PLACE IN TIME AND SPACE – SAINTS, PSYCHOS, SYBILS, FREAKS... GARBAGE 105
poems of alienation, loneliness, and dislocation

AMOR VINCIT OMNIA 121
poems of romance, courtship, and familial love

A GIFT OF PROPHECY 133
poems about seeing history, the future, visions and revisions

© 1971 Gerry Goldberg and George Wright
McClelland and Stewart Limited
The Canadian Publishers
25 Hollinger Road, Toronto 374
Printed and bound in Canada
ISBN 0-7710-3373-7

Stretching away on all sides of most people's awareness are vistas of uncertainty. As we try to pick our individual ways through the necessities of everyday life, the uncertainties press us down.

Always there is the overwhelming question,
phrased in many ways, asking always the same thing:
>	who am I?
>	what am I doing?
>	where am I going?
>	where have I been?
>	why am I here?

Some people find answers that cut through the uncertainty – for them at least. Some try to urge their answers on others. But there are some who live the answers. They may ask those same questions, but their lives unfold certainties in spite of them. Children. They *are* answers. Their lives, lapped in rich sensation, look out on fullness. Inwardly, they see through some trailing vision of richness, too –
>	heaven, Wordsworth called it –
>	Beulah, Blake called it.

Children possess certainty. But they mostly forget it as they change to adults. Some few wise men keep it, or rediscover it. So do idiots and fools and saints have certainty. Maybe animals do too – and maybe machines as well. But maybe not: certainty means a unity of seeing and saying, and a unity of body and spirit. In a word, who has certainty has

>	BEULAH

>>	from Hebrew: married
>>	Isaiah lxii, 4: the land of Israel
>>	*Pilgrim's Progress:* the land of rest
>>	Blake: motherliness, blessedness,
>>		union of maker and made.

SONGS OF INNOCENCE

William Blake

Piping down the valleys wild,
Piping songs of pleasant glee,
On a cloud I saw a child,
And he laughing said to me:

"Pipe a song about a Lamb!"
So I piped with merry chear.
"Piper, pipe that song again;"
So I piped: he wept to hear.

"Drop thy pipe, thy happy pipe;
Sing thy songs of happy chear:"
So I sung the same again,
While he wept with joy to hear.

"Piper, sit thee down and write
In a book that all may read."
So he vanish'd from my sight,
And I pluck'd a hollow reed,

And I made a rural pen,
And I stain'd the water clear,
And I wrote my happy songs
Every child may joy to hear.

THE REASON FOR SKYLARKS

Kenneth Patchen

It was nearly morning when the giant
Reached the tree of children.
Their faces shone like white apples
On the cold dark branches
And their dresses and little coats
Made sodden gestures in the wind.

He did not laugh or weep or stamp
His heavy feet. He set to work at once
Lifting them tenderly down
Into a straw basket which was fixed
By a golden strap to his shoulder.
Only one did he drop – a soft pretty child
Whose hair was the color of watered milk.
She fell into the long grass
And he could not find her
Though he searched until his fingers
Bled and the full light came.

He shook his fist at the sky and called
God a bitter name.

But no answer was made and the giant
Got down on his knees before the tree
And putting his hands about the trunk
Shook
Until all the children had fallen
Into the grass. Then he pranced and stamped
Them to jelly. And still he felt no peace.
He took his half-full basket and set it afire,
Holding it by the handle until
Everything had been burned. He saw now
Two men on steaming horses approaching
From the direction of the world.
And taking a little silver flute
Out of his pocket he played tune
After tune until they came up to him.

The cause of children's ill-temper is the attention which we pay to it; and this is the same whether we grant or refuse their requests. If they once see that we do not want them to cry, they will cry the whole day. The means which we take to quiet them, whether coaxing or threatening, are equally harmful and nearly always ineffective. So long as we notice their tears, they have a reason for continuing; when they see that no one minds them, they will soon improve; for no one, old or young, cares to take useless pains.

Jean-Jacques Rousseau : *Emile*

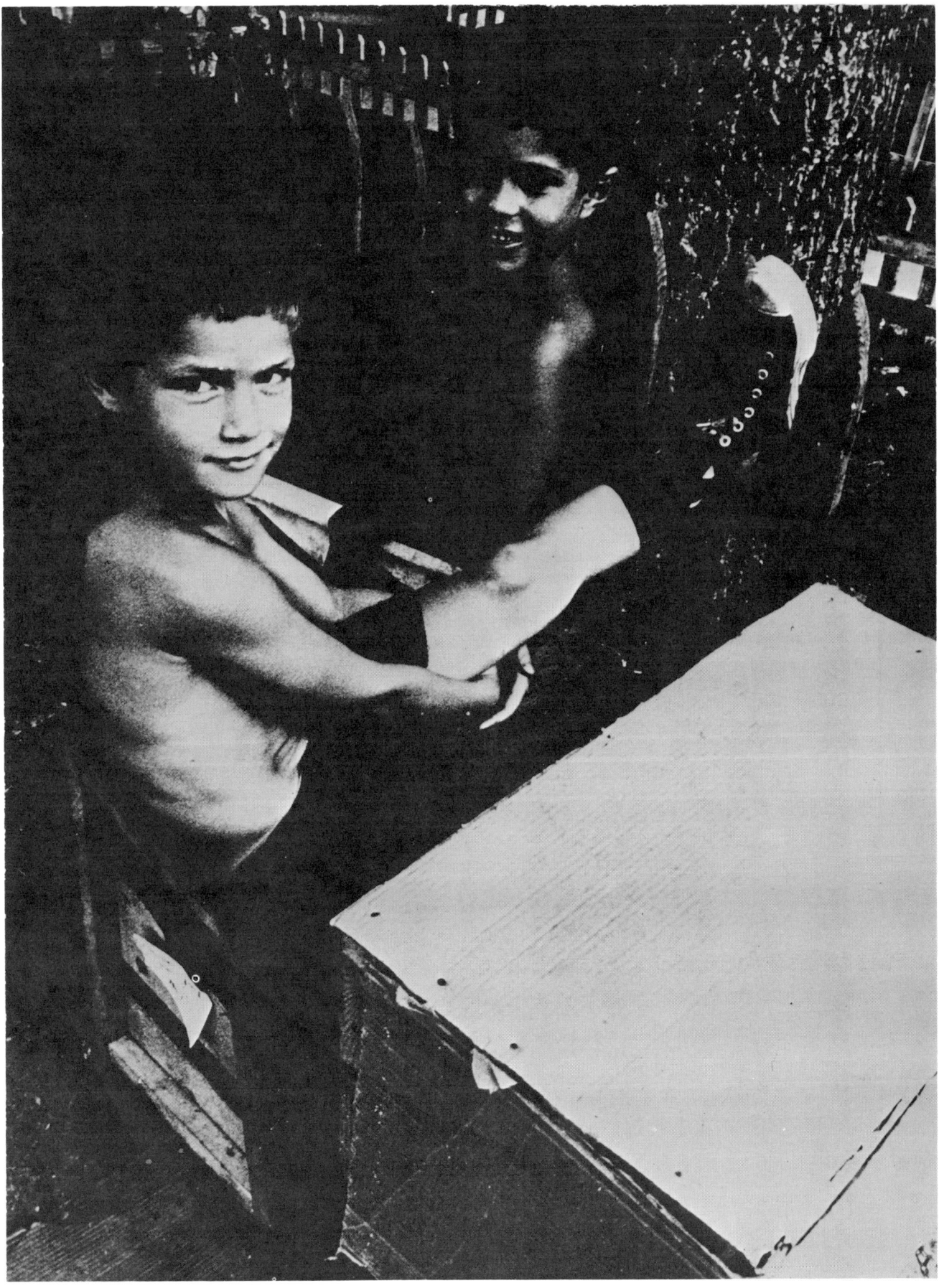

A PRAYER

Bogdan Czaykowski

throw me into a cloud o lord

but do not make me a drop of rain
I do not want to return to earth

throw me into a flower o lord

but do not make me a bee
I would die from an excess of industrious sweetness

throw me into a lake

but do not make me a fish o lord
I would not be able to become cold-blooded

throw me into a forest
like a pine cone on the grass
let no red-haired squirrels find me

throw me into a calm shape of a stone
but not on the pavement of a London street
o lord I worry and bite walls in this alien city

you who turn me over fire
pluck me from flames
and deposit me on a quiet white cloud

DEAR GOD

D. W. K. Cotton

dEar god
    plrase ecscuse mY
    wriTeing to yow wen
    you don evern nO me
    an Pleese doN t½? tHin
    me rOod fow saYin iT
    But i thIngk sumwUn
    uP theyre haS maid
    Asmal mIsstak
    You se iam gEtin@g
    too OR thRe otther
    peples baDD luk
    ass weLlasmI
    Own
        ιotso ff lovE
            deNNis;

INFANT JOY

William Blake

"I have no name:
I am but two days old."
What shall I call thee?
"I happy am,
Joy is my name."
Sweet joy befall thee!

Pretty joy!
Sweet joy but two days old,
Sweet joy I call thee:
Thou dost smile,
I sing the while,
Sweet joy befall thee!

INFANT SORROW

William Blake

My mother groan'd! my father wept.
Into the dangerous world I leapt:
Helpless, naked, piping loud:
Like a fiend hid in a cloud.

Struggling in my father's hands,
Striving against my swadling bands,
Bound and weary I thought best
To sulk upon my mother's breast.

CHANSONS INNOCENTES

e. e. cummings

I

in Just—
spring   when the world is mud
luscious the little
lame balloonman

whistles   far   and wee

and eddieandbill come
running from marbles and
piracies and it's
spring

when the world is puddle-wonderful

the queer
old balloonman whistles
far   and   wee
and bettyandisbel come dancing

from hop-scotch and jump-rope and
it's
spring
and
    the
        goat-footed

balloonMan   whistles
far
and
wee

II

hist   whist
little ghostthings
tip-toe
twinkle-toe

little twitchy
witches and tingling
goblins
hob-a-nob   hob-a-nob

little hoppy happy
toads in tweeds
tweeds
little itchy mousies

with scuttling
eyes   rustle and run   and
hidehidehide
whisk

whisk   look out for the old woman
with the wart on her nose
what she'll do to yer
nobody knows

for she knows the devil   ooch
the devil   ouch
the devil
ach   the great

green
dancing
devil
devil

devil
devil
    wheeEEE

III

Tumbling-hair
      picker of buttercups
                  violets
dandelions
and the big bullying daisies
        through the field wonderful
with eyes a little sorry
Another comes
      also picking flowers

The mind of a child is a mystery and a paradox. Outwardly all clarity and innocence – *O ces voix d'enfants!* – all ignorance and dependence, all rainbow tears and laughter; inwardly the rapt secret communion with realities of another order, with opposites and correspondences of which the golden key is lost to us, with the world of witch and dwarf and monster: the archetypal Fairy-Tale World. A child lives largely in the Unconscious, and is more than a little mad.

    Dunstan and Garlan : *Worlds in the Making*

YOUR CATFISH FRIEND

Richard Brautigan

If I were to live my life
in catfish forms
in scaffolds of skin and whiskers
at the bottom of a pond
and you were to come by
    one evening
when the moon was shining
down into my dark home
and stand there at the edge
    of my affection
and think, "It's beautiful
here by this pond. I wish
    somebody loved me,"
I'd love you and be your catfish
friend and drive such lonely
thoughts from your mind
and suddenly you would be
    at peace,
and ask yourself, "I wonder
if there are any catfish
in this pond? It seems like
a perfect place for them."

GARBAGE MAN

Laurence Josephs

He bears away the rinds of our lives:
He is tides, moon,
And twice each week his reek-
Ing truck sways and smokes
And makes cartoonist aureoles
Of palpable odor above itself in the air.

It is not his fault:

Himself a pure flame, smiling, blond, burning
Our terrible offal,
He is a purity to his wife
Who waits at home with the soap.

And if he comes to her at night
Aglow with the stink of our touch
She makes him clean again.

Like a seed he is,
Bone-white and plucked by choice
From the rotting fruit surrounding.

PORTRAIT

Saint-Denys Garneau
trs. Louis Dudek

He's such a funny kid
He's just like a bird
Already gone

You've got to find him
To seek him out
Once he's there

You've got to mind you don't scare him
He's just like a bird
Or he's like a snail

He only looks at you to give you a kind of hug
Otherwise he does not know what to do with his eyes

Or where to put them
He shuffles them as a peasant shuffles his cap

He has to come toward you
And when he comes to a stop
And if he comes near you
He is no longer there

So it's important to watch him coming
And to love him while he's on the way.

" FORTUNE........."

Lawrence Ferlinghetti

    Fortune
           has its cookies to give out

which is a good thing
        since it's been a long time since

    that summer in Brooklyn
when they closed off the street
    one hot day
      and the

                FIREMEN
                          turned on their hoses
    and all the kids ran out in it
      in the middle of the street
    and there were
        maybe a couple dozen of us
                out there
with the water squirting up
        to the
            sky
        and all over
            us
there was maybe only six of us
        kids altogether
      running around in out
        barefeet and birthday
    suits
      and I remember Molly but then
the firemen stopped squirting their hoses
    all of a sudden and went
      back in
      their firehouse
      and
started playing pinochle again
      just as if nothing
      had ever
        happened
while I remember Molly
        looked at me and

  ran in

because I guess really we were the only ones there

IN IT

George Johnston

The world is a boat and I'm in it
Going like hell with the breeze;
Important people are in it as well
Going with me and the breeze like hell –
It's a kind of a race and we'll win it.
Out of our way, gods, please!

The world is a game and I'm in it
For the little I have, no less;
Important people are in it for more,
They watch the wheel, I watch the door.
Who was the first to begin it?
Nobody knows, but we guess.

The world is a pond and I'm in it,
In it up to my neck;
Important people are in it too,
It's deeper than this, if we only knew;
Under we go, any minute —
A swirl, some bubbles, a fleck . . .

ALL WATCHED OVER BY MACHINES OF LOVING GRACE

Richard Brautigan

I like to think (and
the sooner the better!)
of a cybernetic meadow
where mammals and computers
live together in mutually
programming harmony
like pure water
touching clear sky.

I like to think
    (right now, please!)
of a cybernetic forest
filled with pines and electronics
where deer stroll peacefully
past computers
as if they were flowers
with spinning blossoms.

I like to think
    (it has to be!)
of a cybernetic ecology
where we are free of our labors
and joined back to nature,
returned to our mammal
brothers and sisters,
and all watched over
by machines of loving grace.

THE CHIMNEY SWEEPER

William Blake

A little black thing among the snow,
Crying ' 'weep! 'weep!' in notes of woe!
"Where are thy father & mother? say?"
"They are both gone up to the church to pray.

"Because I was happy upon the heath,
And smil'd among the winter's snow,
They clothed me in the clothes of death,
And taught me to sing the notes of woe.

"And because I am happy & dance & sing,
They think they have done me no injury,
And are gone to praise God & his Priest & King,
Who make up a heaven of our misery."

NIMBLE RAYS OF DAY BRING OXYGEN TO HER BLOOD

Tom Clark

After the sponge bath
Spice cake and coffee
In a sky blue china cup

Tiny clouds float by
Like bits of soap
In a bowl of very blue water

A happy baby sleeps
In a silky chamber
Of my wife's lovely body

A leaf spins itself
The leaf's a roof
Over the trembling flower

Everything's safe there
Because nothing that breathes
Air is alone in the world

As for the older child, the strange cult of the teen-ager is the natural result of this early consumer training. This young human being is led to believe that once he becomes thirteen he becomes a member of the superior race. What the teenager does, wears, wants, and thinks is considered of such prime importance that it must be catered to not only by the outside world but inside the home. The beleaguered parents suddenly find themselves confronted by a dominant and usually hostile herd who take over the house, the meals, the TV set, and the conversation. The adults are unwanted guests in their own home.

Norman Sheffe : *Youth Today*

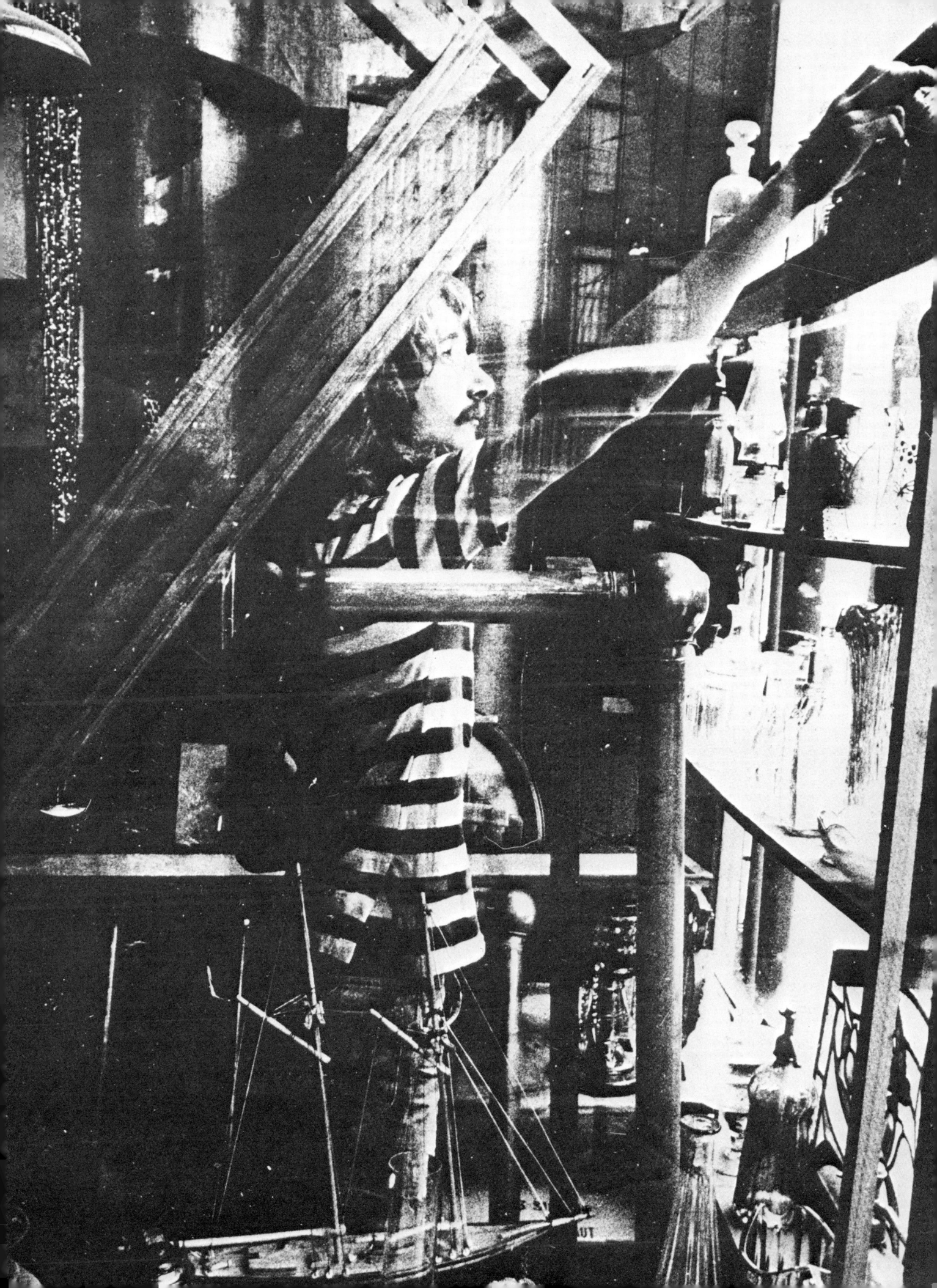

We act every day on the assumption that we know what we are doing. We assume we know our own minds. Reason, we say, is the final guide to human behaviour.

Little do we know.

But we could know a little more with a little less reason.

We could know, for a start, our own minds. We could understand what poets and children and philosophers have known for centuries, that reason, the conscious mind, is only the tip of the iceberg. Most of the mind lies below the surface. Foolish Titanics of reason steaming full of confidence can only smash and sink on the unconscious. Unreason lies below the surface, the vast base of the iceberg, and emerges only when we rest. When we dream. Dreams can reveal the hidden mass of the iceberg. They tell truths that reason cannot find, or that it denies. When someone tells you his dreams, listen, for he is telling you truth. And when he catches his dreams in words, only poetry will do. Read his poetry, for it tells truth.

>And remember your dreams.
>They also tell truth.
>Remember and consider
>WHAT DREAMS TELL.

THE COURT OF THE CRIMSON KING

King Crimson

The rusted chains of prison moons
Are shattered by the sun.
I walk a road, horizons change
The tournament's begun.
The purple piper plays his tune,
The choir softly sing:
Three lullabies in an ancient tongue,
For the court of the crimson king.

The keeper of the city keys
Put shutters on the dreams.
I wait outside the pilgrim's door
With insufficient schemes.
The black queen chants
the funeral march,
The cracked brass bells will ring;
To summon back the fire witch
To the court of the crimson king.

The gardener plants an evergreen
Whilst trampling on a flower.
I chase the wind of a prism ship
To taste the sweet and sour.
The pattern juggler lifts his hand;
The orchestra begin.
As slowly turns the grinding wheel
In the court of the crimson king.

On soft grey mornings widows cry,
The wise men share a joke;
I run to grasp divining signs
To satisfy the hoax.
The yellow jester does not play
But gently pulls the strings
And smiles as the puppets dance
In the court of the crimson king.

DREAMS

Langston Hughes

Hold fast to dreams
For if dreams die
Life is a broken-winged bird
That cannot fly.

Hold fast to dreams
For when dreams go
Life is a barren field
Frozen with snow.

The inner world is our experiencing ourselves, other people, the animate and inanimate world: imagination, dreams, phantasy, and beyond that to ever further reaches of experience.

R. D. Laing : *The Politics of Experience*

The dream is the small hidden door in the deepest and most intimate sanctum of the soul, which opens into that primeval cosmic night that was soul long before there was a conscious ego and will be soul far beyond what a conscious ego could ever reach. For all ego-consciousness is individualized and recognises the single unit in that it separates and distinguishes, and only that which can be related to the ego is seen. This ego-consciousness consists purely of restrictions, even when it stretches to the most distant stars. All consciousness divides; but in dreams we pass into that deeper and more universal, truer and more eternal man who still stands in the dusk of original night, in which he himself was still the whole and the whole was in him, in blind, undifferentiated, pure nature, free from the shackles of the ego. From these all-uniting depths rises the dream, however childish, grotesque, or immoral.

C. G. Jung : *Psychological Reflections*

WOODSTOCK

Joni Mitchell

I came upon a child of God
He was walking along the road
And I asked him, where are you going
And this he told me
I'm going on down to Yasgurs' farm
I'm going to join in a rock'n' roll band
I'm going to camp out on the land
And try an' get my soul free
    We are stardust
    We are golden
    And we've got to get ourselves
    Back to the garden

Then can I walk beside you
I have come here to lose the smog
And I feel to be a cog in something turning
Well maybe it is just the time of year
Of maybe it's the time of man
I don't know who I am
But life is for learning
    We are stardust
    We are golden
    And we've got to get ourselves
    Back to the garden

By the time we got to Woodstock
We were half a million strong
And everywhere there was song and celebration
And I dreamed I saw the bombers
Riding shotgun in the sky
And they were turning into butterflies
Above our nation
    We are stardust
    (Million year old carbon)
    We are golden
    (Caught in the Devil's bargain)
    And we've got to get ourselves
    Back to the garden

In the middle ages English rural villages held May games to welcome in the spring, harvest festivals at which wantonness was encouraged and the renewed fertility of nature celebrated. Woodstock is perhaps our equivalent event.

    Another kind of celebration was led by a "Lord of Misrule," a jester appointed ruler for the day by the townspeople. He functioned as a captain of mischief who mocked majesty and offended the church. For one day, the Lord of Misrule led his followers through sacrilegious rites, deliberately disrupting the social order and mocking authority. The next day, everything would return to normal. In this way, the culture provided a sanctioned release for anarchic and satanic impulses.

Jonathan Eisen : *Altamont*

SYMPATHY FOR THE DEVIL

Mick Jagger and Keith Richards

Please allow me to introduce myself,
I'm a man of wealth and taste
I've been around for a long, Long year
Stolen many a man's soul and faith.

I was around when Jesus Christ
Had his moment of doubt and faith.
I made damn sure that Pilate
Washed his hands and sealed His fate.

Pleased to meet you
Hope you guess my name –
But what's puzzling you
Is the nature of my game.

I stuck around St. Petersburg
When I saw it was time for a change.
I killed the Tzar and his ministers
Anastasia Screamed in vain.

I rode a tank
Held a gen'ral's rank
When the blitzkrieg raged
and the bodies stank.

Pleased to meet you
Hope you guess my name
But what's puzzling you
Is the nature of my game.

I watched with glee
While you kings and queens
Fought for ten decades –
For the Gods they made.

I shouted out:
"Who killed the Kennedys?" –
When after all
It was you and me.

Let me, please, introduce myself
I'm a man of wealth and taste. –

And lay traps for troubadours
Who get killed before
They reach Bombay.

Pleased to meet you
Hope you guess my name
But what's confusing you
Is the nature of my game.

Just as every cop
Is a criminal
And all the sinners,
Saints.

As heads is tails,
Just call me Lucifer
'Cause I'm in need
Of some restraint.

So if you meet me
Have some courtesy –
Have some sympathy
And some taste.

Use all your
Well-learned politesse
Or I'll lay your soul
To waste!

Pleased to meet you,
Hope you guess my name –
But whats puzzling you
Is the nature of my game.

Chest Cee! 'Sdense! Corpo di barragio! you spoof of visibility in a freakfog, of mixed sex cases among goats, hill cat and plain mousey, Bigamy Bob and his old Shanvocht! The Blackfriars treacle plaster outrange be liddled! Therewith was released in that kingsrick of Humidia a poisoning volume of cloud barrage indeed. Yet all they who heard or redelivered are now with that family of bards and Vergobretas himself and the crowd of Caraculacticors as much no more as be they not yet now or had they then not-ever been. Canbe in some future we shall presently here amid those zouave players of Inkermann the mime mumming the mick and his mick miming their maggies, Hilton St Just (Mr. Frank Smith), Ivanne Ste Austelle (Mr. J. F. Jones), Coleman of Lucan taking four parts, a choir of the O'Daley O'Doyles doublesixing the chorus in *Fenn Mac Call and the Serven Feeries of Loch Neach, Galloper Troppler and Hurleyquinn* the zitherer of the past with his merrymen all, zimzim, zimsim.

James Joyce : *Finnegans Wake*

HOW THEY MADE THE GOLEM

John Robert Colombo

To the banks of the Moldau River,
    their lanterns light, their scriptures heavy,
        the three men made their way, the three of them,

The Holy Rabbi of Prague, Judah Loew,
    his brother-in-law, Isaac ben Simson, Cohen,
        and his pupil, Jacob ben Chayim Sasson, Levite.

The night was near midnight. They stopped
    where the banks of the river were of red clay.
        They stood in the darkness, prayed and prepared.

Then each sang the prescribed Psalm:
    "My substance was not hid from thee,
        when I was made in secret, and curiously wrought

in the lowest parts of the earth."
    The Rabbi fingered the time-worn pages
        of the Book of Psalms and the Book of Formation,

selecting the required passages:
    "Thine eyes did see my substance,
        yet being imperfect; and in thy book

all my members were written,
    which in continuance were fashioned,
        when as yet there was none of them.

How precious also are thy thoughts
    unto me, O God! How great is the sum
        of them!" Then, in the earth at his feet,

the bent Rabbi moulded the clay figure
    of my person, making me in length three ells,
        with all the members and measurements of a man.

The Rabbi, the Cohen and the Levite
    stood by my feet regarding my clay face.
        "You are fire." The Cohen walked around me

seven times and sang: "He hewed, as it were
    vast columns out of the great intangible air."
        The charm worked, my clay turned red like fire.

"You are water." The Levite then walked
    around me seven times but the other way,
        singing: "And He bound the twenty-two letters

unto his speech and shewed him all
    the mysteries of them." Water flowed from me,
        hair sprouted, toes and fingers grew crude nails.

"You are air." The Rabbi bent down to me
    and inserted the parchmented name, the Shem,
        deep into my clay mouth, and together they prayed:

"And He breathed into his nostrils
    the breath of life; and the man became
        a living soul." With that I opened my eyes.

I saw them there, heard the Rabbi's command:
    "Stand up!" And I stood up, a dumb stranger.
        They handed me their sexton's dirty garments.

"You are Joseph," the Rabbi said.
    "You will destroy the entire Jew-baiting
        company." I nodded, for I had no powers of speech.

The three of them led me away as a fourth.
    "A dumb creature of magicians," Isaac said.
        "A creation, like Adam," Jacob said. But I thought:

"How precious also are thy thoughts
    unto me, O God! How great is the sum
        of them!" And they led me into the city of Prague.

It is said that the origin of the story goes back to the seventeenth century. According to the lost formulas of the Kabbalah, a rabbi (Judah Loew ben Bezabel) made an artificial man – the foresaid Golem – so that he would ring the bells and take over all the menial tasks of the synagogue.

He was not a man exactly, and had only a sort of dim, half-conscious vegetative existence. By the power of a magic tablet which was placed under his tongue and which attracted the free sidereal energies of the universe, this existence lasted during the daylight hours.

One night before evening prayer, the rabbi forgot to take the tablet out of the Golem's mouth, and the creature fell into a frenzy, running out into the dark alleys of the ghetto and knocking down those who got in his way, until the rabbi caught up with him and removed the tablet.

At once the creature fell lifeless. . . .

Gustav Meyrink : *Der Golem*

Golem (gó lim), *n*. Heb., orig., embryo; later, monster (hence Yid. sense "dolt"); in Jewish legend, a man artificially created by cabalistic rites; robot; automaton.

. . . that country where it is always turning late in the year. That country where the hills are fog and the rivers are mist; where noons go quickly, dusks and twilights linger, and midnights stay. That country composed in the main of cellars, sub-cellars, coal-bins, closets, attics, and pantries faced away from the sun. That country whose people are autumn people, thinking only autumn thoughts. Whose people passing at night on the empty walks sound like rain. . . .

Ray Bradbury : *The October Country*

ONLY CHILD

Edwin Brock

At the age of eight I practised levitation:
lay in bed and willed myself six inches
from the ceiling. Underneath me
the ground was dead; some pale-faced

boy slept in my bed; I would have known
if he had been my brother. Regularly
at night my parents came to this one,
kissed him carefully and curled the clothes

about him. I was not aware of love
or anything like that: we did not fight
this boy and I, nor did I begrudge him
their attention. Call it what you like,

that nightly jaunt I took, analyse it
as you will, there must have been
some benefit I gained from it — otherwise
I'd have come down long ago.

THE WITCH

Gillian Pursey

The witch is an ugly creature.
Her clothes are tattered and torn.
She has hair as stiff as wire
And teeth as black as liquorice.
Her face has wrinkles like cracks in mountains.
Her lips are cold as stone.
Her eyes are like pebbles washed in a stream.
Her nose is sharp as a nail,
Her chin crooked like a twig.
Her fingers are like a spindly tree.
She laughs as she sails about on her broomstick
Because her feet are as big as boats.

Long, crooked shadows fell over the river and muffled sounds crept along the murky banks. In the creaking of the thick beech branches, in the rustling of the willows trailing their leaves in the water, I heard the utterances of the mysterious beings of whom Olga had spoken. They took on peculiar shapes, serpentine and peaked of face, having a bat's head and a snake's body. And they coiled themselves around a man's legs, drawing his will to live out of him until he sat down on the ground, in search of a slumber from which there was no awakening.

Jerzy Kosinski : *The Painted Bird*

She called me the Black One. From her I learned for the first time that I was possessed by an evil spirit, which crouched in me like a mole in a deep burrow, and of whose presence I was unaware. Such a person as I, possessed of this evil spirit, could be recognized by his bewitched black eyes which did not blink when they gazed at the bright clear eyes. Hence, Olga declared, I could stare at other people and unknowingly cast a spell over them.

This evil spirit which dwelled in me attracted by its very nature other mysterious beings. Phantoms drifted around me. A phantom is silent, reticent, and is rarely seen. Yet it is persistent: it trips people in fields and forests, peeks into huts, can turn itself into a vicious cat or rabid dog, and moans when enraged. At midnight it turns into hot tar.

Ghosts are attracted to an evil spirit. They are persons long dead, condemned to eternal damnation, returning to life only at full moon, having superhuman powers, with eyes always turned mournfully eastward.

Vampires, perhaps the most harmful of these intangible threats because they often assume human form, are also drawn to a possessed person. Vampires are people who were drowned without having first been baptized or who were abandoned by their mothers. They grow to the age of seven in the water or in the forests, whereupon they take human form again. . . .

Jerzy Kosinski : *The Painted Bird*

THE SORCERER

A. J. M. Smith

There is a sorcerer in Lachine
Who for a small fee will put a spell
On my beloved, who has sea-green
Eyes, and on my doting self as well.

He will transform us, if we like, to goldfish:
We shall swim in a crystal bowl,
And the bright water will go swish
Over our naked bodies; we shall have no soul.

In the morning the syrupy sunshine
Will dance on our tails and fins.
I shall have her then all for mine,
And Father Lebeau will hear no more of her sins.

Come along, good sir, change us into goldfish.
I would put away intellect and lust,
Be but a red gleam in a crystal dish,
But kin of the trembling ocean, not of the dust.

THE WORLD UPSIDE DOWN

Onitsura

The trout leaps high –
   below him, in the river bottom,
     clouds fly by.

DREAMPOEM

Roger McGough

in a corner of my bedroom
    grew a tree
    a happy tree
    my own tree
its leaves were soft
    like flesh
and its birds sang poems for me
then
    without warning
two men
    with understanding smiles
and axes
    made out of forged excuses
came and chopped it down
either   yesterday
    or the day before
i think it was the day before

YOUNG WOMAN AT A WINDOW

William Carlos Williams

She sits with
tears on

her cheek
her cheek on

her hand
the child

in her lap
his nose

pressed
to the glass

THE REASON I WRITE

Leonard Cohen

The reason I write
is to make something
as beautiful as you are

When I'm with you
I want to be the kind of hero
I wanted to be
when I was seven years old
a perfect man
who kills

THE ORIGIN OF BASEBALL

Kenneth Patchen

Someone had been walking in and out
Of the world without coming
To much decision about anything.
The sun seemed too hot most of the time.
There weren't enough birds around
And the hills had a silly look
When he got on top of one.
The girls in heaven, however, thought
Nothing of asking to see his watch
Like you would want someone to tell
A joke – "Time," they'd say, "what's
That mean – time?", laughing with the edges
Of their white mouths, like a flutter of paper
In a madhouse. And he'd stumble over
General Sherman or Elizabeth B.
Browning, muttering, "Can't you keep
Your big wings out of the aisle?" But down
Again, there'd be millions of people without
Enough to eat and men with guns just
Standing there shooting each other.

So he wanted to throw something
And he picked up a baseball.

RETURN

Lou Lipsitz

No moon.
My boots crunch on the iced-over path.
The woods are still.
I have nowhere to go.

Then from a dark place
you jump out and throw yourself on my shoulders.
You've come back.

I will carry you,
strange rider.

RIDE A WILD HORSE

Hannah Kahn

Ride a wild horse
with purple wings
striped yellow and black
except his head
which must be red.

Ride a wild horse
against the sky
hold tight to his wings ...
Before you die
whatever else you leave undone,
once, ride a wild horse
into the sun.

A DREAM DEFERRED

Langston Hughes

What happens to a dream deferred?

   Does it dry up
   Like a raisin in the sun?
   Or fester like a sore –
   And then run?
   Does it stink like rotten meat
   Or crust and sugar over –
   like a syrupy sweet?

   Maybe it just sags
   like a heavy load.

   Or does it explode?

To see a World in a Grain of Sand
And a Heaven in a Wild Flower,
Hold Infinity in the palm of your hand
And Eternity in an hour.

       William Blake : *Auguries of Innocence*

MARINA

T. S. Eliot

*Quis hic locus, quae
regio, quae mundi plaga?*

What seas what shores what grey rocks and what islands
What water lapping the bow
And scent of pine and the woodthrush singing through the fog
What images return
O my daughter.

Those who sharpen the tooth of the dog, meaning
Death
Those who glitter with the glory of the hummingbird, meaning
Death
Those who sit in the stye of contentment, meaning
Death
Those who suffer the ecstasy of the animals, meaning
Death

Are become unsubstantial, reduced by a wind,
A breath of pine, and the woodsong fog
By this grace dissolved in place

What is this face, less clear and clearer
The pulse in the arm, less strong and stronger –
Given or lent? more distant than stars and nearer than the eye

Whispers and small laughter between leaves and hurrying feet
Under sleep, where all the waters meet.

Bowsprit cracked with ice and paint cracked with heat.
I made this, I have forgotten
And remember.
The rigging weak and the canvas rotten
Between one June and another September.
Made this unknowing, half conscious, unknown, my own.
The garboard strake leaks, the seams need caulking.
This form, this face, this life
Living to live in a world of time beyond me; let me
Resign my life for this life, my speech for that unspoken,
The awakened, lips parted, the hope, the new ships.

What seas what shores what granite islands towards my timbers
And woodthrush calling through the fog
My daughter.

What an abyss of uncertainty, whenever the mind feels that some part of it has strayed beyond its own borders; when it, the seeker, is at the same time the dark region through which it must go seeking, where all its equipment will avail it nothing. Seek? More than that: create. It is face to face with something which does not so far exist, to which it alone can give reality and substance, which it alone can bring into the light of day.

Marcel Proust : *Remembrance of Times Past*

TRUE TO A DREAM

Donald Petersen

And the curtains, the lamp,
The rose-papered wall,
The familiar cramp
Of books in the rack,
Would fade; he would fall
Through a slumbrous abyss
To a great zodiac
Where the lions hiss,
Where the master swings
A nine-tailed whip
Or the bluebird sings
In a private arbor
Or a wonderful ship
Has the sky for a harbor

And when it was past
All that he saw
Was darkness and vast
Confusions of vapor,
And rubbed his eyes raw.
And when he awoke,
The book-laden shelf
And the old rose-paper
Appeared the same
And he fancied himself
Cut off at a stroke,
In a trice undone,
For as quick as it came
The show passed on.

And the persons he met,
Were brave but sad.
One paused by the bed
But could not talk.
Another one had
A limp in his walk.
There was a lone
Boy on a crutch
An heir to a throne
Was locked out of touch.
And the princess was pining
As princesses must
And everything shining
Began to rust.

And hour after hour,
Yet always true,
To the one highest tower
The boy withdrew.
And true to a dream
That opens and closes,
He ruled supreme,
Suppressing the roses
That mounted the wall,
Until in a bold,
Deliberate choice
He relinquished his hold
At the faraway call
Of a downstairs voice.

THURSDAY

William Carlos Williams

I have had my dream – like others –
and it has come to nothing, so that
I remain now carelessly
with feet planted on the ground
and look up at the sky –
feeling my clothes about me,
the weight of my body in my shoes,
the rim of my hat, air passing in and out
at my nose – and decide to dream no more.

The dream is specifically the utterance of the unconscious. We may call consciousness the daylight realm of the human psyche, and contrast it with the nocturnal realm of unconscious psychic activity, which we apprehend as dreamlike phantasy.

C. G. Jung : *Psychological Reflections*

The brain is a billion lens motion picture camera shooting and coordinating billions of frames a second. The "imprint" system is one of these frames – stopped – upon which man's perception and symbolic thinking develops.

Man's mind imposes upon the variegated flow of energy one static model – years out of date, kept current only by the slow process of conditioning and association . . . What happens outside or inside, we perceive in terms of our mental imprinting system. We live in a dead world – cut off from the flow of life and energy.

Timothy Leary : "Languages: Energy Systems Sent and Received"

Itinerant man.
Wandering man.
Searching man.

Every person has felt the passage of change. As we live we change. Change, in fact, is living, stillness is death. But through it all, it is in the hearts of most people to expect, somewhere, a penultimate stillness – achievement, success, happiness, fulfilment, wisdom, however we choose to see it or name it.

> We hope to arrive some day.
> But in the meantime, we live and look. Searching becomes a way of living.

Or put in another way, the quest is life.

> A voyage.
> A journey.

And everyone is a stranger, as Albert Camus saw,
> or a sailor, as Joseph Conrad saw,
> or a pilgrim, as Chaucer saw.

They all saw aspects of that same elemental vision. So persistent has been the notion of life as a journey that many philosophers have seen it as an archetype, a basic human way of seeing. And most of us, people of all races and times, pass along the way. We live and change and hope for the end of change somewhere before the end of life.

> Searching man.
> Wandering man.
> Itinerant man.
> HOMO VIATOR.

BEDTIME STORY

George Macbeth

(A giant ant is telling a bedtime story to one of its children. The story is the legend of how the last man was accidentally wiped out by a Mission Patrol wishing to help him.)

Long long ago when the world was a wild place
Planted with bushes and peopled by apes, our
Mission Brigade was at work in the jungle.
    Hard by the Congo

Once, when a foraging detail was active
Scouting for green-fly, it came on a grey man, the
Last living man, in the branch of a baobab
    Stalking a monkey.

Earlier men had disposed of, for pleasure
Creatures whose names we scarcely remember –
Zebra, rhinoceros, elephants, wart-hog,
    Lion, rats, deer. But

After the wars had extinguished the cities
Only the wild ones were left, half-naked
Near the Equator: and here was the last one,
    starved for a monkey.

By then the Mission Brigade had encountered
Hundreds of such men: and their procedure,
History tells us, was only to feed them:
    Find them and feed them;

Those were the orders. And this was the last one.
Nobody knew that he was, but he was. Mud
Caked on his flat grey flanks. He was crouched, half-
    armed with a shaved spear.

Glinting beneath broad leaves. When their jaws cut
Swathes through the bark and he saw fine teeth shine,
Round eyes roll round and forked arms waver
    Huge as the rough trunks

Over his head, he was frightened. Our workers
Marched through the Congo before he was born, but
This was the first time perhaps that he'd seen one.
    Staring in the hot still

Silence, he crouched there: then jumped. With a long swing
Down from his branch, he had angled his spear too
Quickly, before they could hold him, and hurled it
    hard at the soldier

Leading the detail. How could he know the Queen's
Orders were only to help him? The soldier
Winced when the tipped spear pricked him. Unsheathing his
    Sting was a reflex.

Later the Queen was informed. There were no more
Men. An impetuous soldier had killed off,
Purely by chance, the penultimate primate.
    When she was certain,

Squadrons of workers were fanned through the Congo
Detailed to bring back the man's picked bones to be
Sealed in the archives in amber. I'm quite sure
    Nobody found them.

After the most industrious search, though.
Where had the bones gone? Over the earth, dear,
Ground by the teeth of the termites, blown by the
    Wind, like the dodo's.

    Where is he now? Titus the Abdicator? Come out of the shadows, traitor, and stand upon the wild brink of my brain!
    He cannot know, wherever he may be, that through the worm-pocked doors and fractured walls, through windows bursted, gaping, soft with rot, a storm is pouring into Gormenghast. It scours the flagstones; churns the sullen moat, prizes the long beams from their crumbling joists; and howls! He cannot know, as every moment passes, the multifarious action of his home.
    A rocking horse, festooned with spiders' rigging, sways where there's no one in a gusty loft.
    He cannot know that as he turns his head, three armies of black ants, in battle order, are passing now like shades across the spines of a great library.
    Has he forgotten where the breastplates burn like blood within the eyelids, and great domes reverberate to the coughing of a rat?
    He only knows that he has left behind him, on the far side of the skyline, something inordinate; something brutal; something tender; something half real; something half dream; half of his heart; half of himself.
    And all the while the far hyena laughter.

                                          Mervyn Peake : *Titus Alone*

NOT REACHING A LAKE

Lou Lipsitz

I fall over a rock. My left foot that was healing
is twisted again.
        Lake, that I hoped to reach this morning, I cannot
           make it.
        I am lame
           and will have to do without you.

I rest on the forest floor.
Sun edges carefully into the woods. A perfect hour.
Birds burst into the air, calling. A cardinal perches near me
and I lie still, watching him preening and looking for insects.
He is undisturbed.

Elsewhere, the lame world drags itself on.

WOULD YOU TRADE YOUR PAIN

John Bruce

Would you trade your pain
For a part of my death?
If brothers were gentler than this
Would they feed us their share of the light?

Has all death got this wet mouth
And dry skin as though washed
Over and over and towelled
Just too clean as plaster?

Oh, Jesus, yes, it's pure like that
And afterwards the sound of it
Is like the colour of ashes
Rubbed between the palms.

CIRCLES IN THE SAND

Carl Sandburg

The white man drew a small circle in the sand
and told the red man, "This is what the Indian
knows," and drawing a big circle around the
small one, "This is what the white man knows."
The Indian took the stick and swept an immense
ring around both circles: "This is where the
white man and the red man know nothing."

"I have killed many men and loved many women and much meat. I have also been hungry, and I thank you for that and for the added sweetness that food has when you receive it after such time.

"You make all things and direct them in their ways, O Grandfather, and now you have decided that the Human Beings will soon have to walk a new road. Thank you for letting us win once before that happened. Even if my people must eventually pass from the face of the earth, they will live on in whatever men are fierce and strong. So that when women see a man who is proud and brave and vengeful, even if he has a white face, they will cry: "That is a Human Being!"

                Thomas Berger : *Little Big Man*

Yes! in the sea of life enisled,
With echoing straits between us thrown,
Dotting the shoreless watery wild,
We mortals millions live alone.

                Matthew Arnold : "To Marguerite"

We are bemused and crazed creatures, strangers to our true selves, to one another, and to the spiritual and material world – mad, even, from an ideal standpoint we can glimpse but not adopt.

                R. D. Laing : *The Politics of Experience*

CHRIST CLIMBED DOWN

Lawrence Ferlinghetti

Christ climbed down
from His bare Tree
this year
and ran away to where
there were no rootless Christmas trees
hung with candycanes and breakable stars

Christ climbed down
from His bare Tree
this year
and ran away to where
there were no gilded Christmas trees
and no tinsel Christmas trees
and no tinfoil Christmas trees
and no pink plastic Christmas trees
and no gold Christmas trees
and no black Christmas trees
and no powderblue Christmas trees
hung with electric candles
and encircled by tin electric trains
and clever cornball relatives

Christ climbed down
from His bare Tree
this year
and ran away to where
no intrepid Bible salesmen
covered the territory
in two-tone cadillacs
and where no Sears Roebuck creches
complete with plastic babe in manger
arrived by parcel post
the babe by special delivery
and where no televised Wise Men
praised the Lord Calvert Whiskey

Christ climbed down
from His bare Tree
this year
and ran away to where

no fat handshaking stranger
in a red flannel suit
and a fake white beard
went around passing himself off
as some sort of North Pole saint
crossing the desert to Bethlehem
Pennsylvania
in a Volkswagon sled
drawn by rollicking Adirondack reindeer
with German names
and bearing sacks of Humble Gifts
from Saks Fifth Avenue
for everybody's imagined Christ child

Christ climbed down
from His bare Tree
this year
and ran away to where
no Bing Crosby carollers
groaned of a tight Christmas
and where no Radio City angels
iceskated wingless
thru a winter wonderland
into a jinglebell heaven
daily at 8:30
with Midnight Mass matinees

Christ climbed down
from His bare Tree
this year
and softly stole away into
some anonymous Mary's womb again
where in the darkest night
of everybody's anonymous soul
He awaits again
an unimaginable
and impossibly
Immaculate Reconception
the very craziest
of Second Comings

AVARICE AND AMBITION ONLY WERE THE FIRST BUILDERS OF TOWNS AND FOUNDERS OF EMPIRE

Kenneth Patchen

They said, go to, let us build us a city and a tower whose top may reach unto Heaven, and let us make us a name, lest we be scattered abroad upon the face of the earth (Genesis XI:4). What was the beginning of this city? What was it but a concourse of thieves, and a sanctuary of criminals? It was justly named by the augury of no less than twelve vultures, and the founder cemented his walls with the steaming blood of his only brother. Not unlike to this was the beginning even of the first town in the world, and such is the original sin of most cities: Their actual increase daily with their age and growth; the more people, the more wicked all of them; everyone brings in his part to inflame the contagion, which becomes at last so universal and so strong, that no precepts can be sufficient preservatives, nor anything secure our safety, but flight from among the infected. To spread our own disease

They scatter me from church to gutter.
They smear their doings over my hands.
I am lifted out of wombs
and never put back anywhere . . .
I look up from the grass and down from the cathedral.
They honor me with the stuff of dogs.
They place my body down and fill themselves.
I smile from the confessional and frown on the battlemount.
They offer me their wives
And kill my firstborn . . .
I am grown in their hovels like a vegetable that can be eaten.

They won't wash off my dirt.
They put me in parades and distribute pieces of my corpse.
They honor me with statues and seal me in the hardening mold.
I could never build a man
And I have come here to worship . . .

I have only this one wreath.
There is only one grave anywhere.
I am standing open.
You must not lower your eyes.

I want them all to know me.
I want my breath to go over them.
They should withhold nothing from me.
I am a respecter of dirt.
This is your house, you say. Then show
Yourself! I have not been on earth
Long enough to know about you. This
Collection of ills and organs means nothing
To me. Everybody gets a whack at them.
Tell me what you do inside there. I want
All your pain. I want to walk around where
You are. There is no war between us.

And every now and again somebody sneaks up and
Boots the hell out of you
But I could never build one of these curious things
And I have come here because of that simplicity
Is it so very dark in there, brothers?
Does it hurt all the time?
Does it rain without any end at all?
Are the same monsters in your streets?
Why have you nailed up your doors, brothers?
And every now and again something looks down and
Smears the doings of God over our murderous hands

I should like to pray now if I can stay out of a trench to do it
There is no war between us, brothers.
There is only one war anywhere.

Truth can never be told so as to be understood, and not believ'd.

William Blake : *Marriage of Heaven and Hell*

Does not everything happen as though this ruined universe turned relentlessly upon whomever claimed that he could settle down in it to the extent of erecting a permanent dwelling there for himself?

Gabriel Marcel : *Homo Viator*

Terror, grief, and desolation –
Hut, tup, thrup, fo! –
Come to every Earthling nation!
Hut, tup, thrup, fo! –
Earth eat fire! Earth wear chains!
Hut, tup, thrup, fo!
Break Earth's spirit, spill Earth's brains!
Hut, tup, thrup, fo!
Scream! Tup, thrup, fo!
Bleed! Tup, thrup, fo!
Die! Tup, thrup, fo!
Dooooooooooommmmmmmmm.

Kurt Vonnegut : *Sirens of Titan*

ON TOP OF MILAN CATHEDRAL

Ralph Gustafson

Four thousand saints surround me.
My soul is utterly taken by the man
Selling Cokes from a red refrigerator
On the roof of Milan Cathedral.

I am unused to this commercial society
And walk the lead slope near the balustrade
With mine eyes as if they did not see
The solid wooden booth and the counter

But it is no use: the sun broils
And the cathedral is a million dollar failure.
The Virgin Mary and Christ holding
Open like a miraculous cardiac his bleeding

Heart, are for sale in coloured plaster.
There are assorted bottlecaps
Amongst the sleeves of straws and paper.
I have sat amid angels and pinnacles

Being hot and closed mine eyes to commerce.
The man's wife argues about money
But it is in a dialect beyond my comprehension.
I think of the indeterminate profit

Of martyrs and the shareholders in a better Company.
I shall unroll the end of a Verichrome
And feed it into my Kodak before
The host risen about me is substantial.

TIME LAUGHED . . .

M. Broderson

Time laughed into my eyes with head so thrown back, so tilted, with such biting and bitter chuckles that through my eye there passed a lightning tremor; and like a splinter of that ringing laughter, madness pierced me through and through.

I heard within me a wild dog-like whining growing ever more pitiless, savage, villainous: "Why! – am I my brother's keeper?" And from the heights swooped down a lightning-stroke – a rope to strangle the hidden withered happiness.

Water, water every where,
And all the boards did shrink;
Water, water, every where,
Nor any drop to drink.

The very deep did rot: O Christ!
That ever this should be!
Yea, slimy things did crawl with legs
Upon the slimy sea.

Samuel Taylor Coleridge : *"Rime of the Ancient Mariner"*

THE SEAFARER: *From the Anglo-Saxon*

Ezra Pound

May I for my own self song's truth reckon,
Journey's jargon, how I in harsh days
Hardship endured oft.
Bitter breast-cares have I abided,
Known on my keel many a care's hold,
And dire sea-surge, and there I oft spent
Narrow nightwatch nigh the ship's head
While she tossed close to cliffs. Coldly afflicted,
My feet were by frost benumbed.
Chill its chains are; chafing sighs
Hew my heart round and hunger begot
Mere-weary mood. Lest man know not
That he on dry land loveliest liveth,
List how I, care-wretched, on ice-cold sea,
Weathered the winter, wretched outcast
Deprived of my kinsmen;
Hung with hard ice-flakes, where hail-scur flew,
There I heard naught save the harsh sea
And ice-cold wave, at whiles the swan cries,
Did for my games the gannet's clamour,
Sea fowls' loudness was for me laughter,
The mews' singing all my mead-drink.
Storms, on the stone-cliffs beaten, fell on the stern
In icy feathers, full oft the eagle screamed
With spray on his pinion.

          Not any protector
May make merry man faring needy.
This he little believes, who aye in winsome life
Abides 'mid burghers some heavy business,
Wealthy and wine-flushed, how I weary oft
Must bide above brine.
Neareth nightshade, snoweth from north,
Frost froze the land, hail fell on earth then,
Corn of the coldest. Nathless there knocketh now
The heart's thought that I on high streams
The salt-wavy tumult traverse alone.
Moaneth alway my mind's lust
That I fare forth, that I afar hence
Seek out a foreign fastness.
For this there's no mood-lofty man over earth's midst,
Not though he be given his good, but will have in his youth greed;
Nor his deed to the daring, nor his kind to the faithful
But shall have his sorrow for sea-fare
Whatever his lord will.
He hath not heart for harping, nor in ring-having
Nor winsomeness to wife, nor world's delight
Nor any whit else save the wave's slash,
Yet longing comes upon him to fare forth on the water.
Bosque taketh blossom, cometh beauty of berries,
Fields to fairness, land fares brisker,
All this admonisheth man eager of mood,
The heart turns to travel so that he then thinks
On flood-ways to be far departing.
Cuckoo calleth with gloomy crying,
He singeth summerward, bodeth sorrow,
The bitter heart's blood. Burgher knows not –
He the prosperous man – what some perform
Where wandering them widest draweth.
So that but now my heart burst from my breastlock,
My mood 'mid the mere-flood,
Over the whale's acre, would wander wide.
On earth's shelter cometh oft to me,
Eager and ready, the crying lone-flyer,
Whets for the whale-path the heart irresistibly,
O'er tracks of ocean; seeing that anyhow
My lord deems to me this dead life
On loan and on land, I believe not
That any earth-weal eternal standeth
Save there be somewhat calamitous
That, ere a man's tide go, turn it to twain.
Disease or oldness or sword-hate
Beats out the breath from doom-gripped body.
And for this, every earl whatever, for those speaking after –
Laud of the living, boasteth some last word,
That he will work ere he pass onward,
Frame on the fair earth 'gainst foes his malice,
Daring ado, ...
So that all men shall honour him after
And his laud beyond them remain 'mid the English,
Aye, for ever, a lasting life's-blast,
Delight 'mid the doughty.... Days little durable,
And all arrogance of earthen riches,
There come now no kings nor Cæsars
Nor gold-giving lords like those gone.
Howe'er in mirth most magnified,
Whoe'er lived in life most lordliest,
Drear all this excellence, delights undurable!
Waneth the watch, but the world holdeth.
Tomb hideth trouble. The blade is layed low.
Earthly glory ageth and seareth.
No man at all going the earth's gait,
But age fares against him, his face paleth,
Grey-haired he groaneth, knows gone companions,
Lordly men, are to earth o'ergiven,
Nor may he then the flesh-cover, whose life ceaseth,
Nor eat the sweet nor feel the sorry,
Nor stir hand nor think in mid heart,
And though he strew the grave with gold,
His born brothers, their buried bodies
Be an unlikely treasure hoard.

THE GAME

Saint-Denys Garneau
trs. F. R. Scott

Don't bother me I'm terribly busy

A child is starting to build a village
It's a city, a county
And who knows
        Soon the universe.

He's playing

These wooden blocks are houses he moves about and castles
This board is the sign of a sloping roof
        not at all bad to look at
It's no small thing to know the place where the road of cards
        will turn
This could change completely
        The course of the river
Because of the bridge which makes so beautiful a reflection
        on the water of the carpet
It's easy to have a tall tree
And to put a mountain underneath
        so it'll be high up

Joy of playing! Paradise of liberties!
But above all don't put your foot in the room
One never knows what might be in this corner
Or whether you are not going to crush the favourite
        among the invisible flowers

This is my box of toys
Full of words for weaving marvellous patterns
For uniting separating matching
Now the unfolding of the dance
And soon a clear burst of the laughter
That one thought had been lost

A gentle flip of the finger
And the star
Which hung carelessly
At the end of too flimsy a thread of light
Falls and makes rings in the water

Of love and tenderness who would dare to doubt
But not two cents of respect for the established order
Or for politeness and this precious discipline
A levity and practices fit to scandalise grown up people
He arranges words for you as if they were simple songs
And in his eyes one can read his mischievous pleasure
At knowing that under the words he moves everything about
And plays with the mountains
As if they were his very own.
He turns the room upside down and truly we've lost our way
As if it was fun just to fool people.

And yet in his left eye when the right is smiling
A supernatural importance is imparted to the leaf of a tree
As if this could be of great significance
Had as much weight in his scales
As the war of Ethiopia
In England's.

We are not book-keepers

Everyone can see a green dollar bill
But who can see through it
        except a child
Who like him can see through it with full freedom
Without being in the least hampered by it
        or its limitations
Or by its value of exactly one dollar

For he sees through this window thousands of marvellous toys
And has no wish to choose between these treasures
Nor desire nor necessity
Not he
For his eyes are wide open to take everything.

You have navigated with raging soul far from the paternal home, passing beyond the sea's double rocks, and you now inhabit a foreign land.

    Albert Camus : *Myth of Sisyphus*

You never know what is enough unless you know what is more than enough.

    William Blake : *Marriage of Heaven and Hell*

GAUTAMA IN THE DEER PARK AT BENARES

Kenneth Patchen

In a hut of mud and fire
Sits this single man – "Not to want
Money, to want a life in the world,
To want no trinkets on my name" –
And he was rich; his life lives where
Death cannot go; his honor stares
At the sun.

The fawn sleeps. The little winds
Ruffle the earth's green hair. It is
Wonderful to live. My sword rusts
In the pleasant rain. I shall not think
Anymore. I touch the face of my friend;
He shows his dirty teeth as he scratches
At a flea – and we grin. It is warm
And the rice stirs usefully in our bellies.

The fawn raises its head – the sun floods
Its soft eye with the kingdoms of life –
I think we should all go to sleep now,
And not care anymore.

Siddhartha gave his clothes to a poor Brahmin on the road and only retained his loincloth and earth-colored unstitched cloak. He only ate once a day and never cooked food. He fasted fourteen days. He fasted twenty-eight days. The flesh disappeared from his legs and cheeks. Strange dreams were reflected in his enlarged eyes. The nails grew long on his thin fingers and a dry, bristly beard appeared on his chin. His glance became icy when he encountered women; his lips curled with contempt when he passed through a town of well-dressed people. He saw businessmen trading, princes going to the hunt, mourners weeping over their dead, prostitutes offering themselves, doctors attending the sick, priests deciding the day for sowing, lovers making love, mothers soothing their children – and all were not worth a passing glance, everything lied, stank of lies; they were all illusions of sense, happiness and beauty. All were doomed to decay. The world tasted bitter. Life was pain.

Hermann Hesse : *Siddhartha*

One must not count too much on God, but perhaps God counts on us.

Pauwels and Bergier : *The Morning of the Magicians*

We have come a long way together, you and I, since first we set out upon this strange, uncertain pilgrimage. We picked our way through the Slough of Despond and found that the bogs and quagmires were but figments of our imagination; we have visited the City of Despair and found it walled in only by its own fantasies of Space and Time; we have confronted the Lions of Automata and discovered them to be ephemera, the mirror image of our own minds; we have traversed the valley of Paradise and eaten of its strange Fruit, Leisure. Now, we have but a little further to go and our Pilgrimage will be at an end. We must cross the Delectable Mountains. They may seem far away, shimmering there; but that is an accident of our eyesight. They really are right here under our feet, if we will but look. Like the Chinese journey of a thousand miles, we shall approach them one step at a time. Shall we go? Now?

Don Fabun : *Dynamics of Change*

I believe future generations will think of our times as the age of wholeness: when the walls began to fall; when the fragments began to be related to each other; when man . . . learned to realize his brokenness and his great talent for creating ties that bind him together again; . . . when he began to realize his infinite possibilities even as he sees more clearly his limitations; . . . when he learned never to let any power or dictator cut his ties to the great reservoir of knowledge and wisdom without which he would quickly lose his human status; when he learned to live a bit more comfortably with time and space; when he learned to accept his need of God and the law that he cannot use Him, to accept his need of his fellow men and the law that he cannot use them, either; when he learned that "what is impenetrable to us really exists," and always there will be need of the dream, the belief, the wonder, the faith.

To believe in something not yet proved and to underwrite it with our lives; it is the only way we can leave the future open. Man, surrounded by facts, permitting himself no surmise, no intuitive flash, no great hypothesis, no risk, is in a locked cell. Ignorance cannot seal the mind and imagination more surely. To find the point where hypothesis and fact meet; the delicate equilibrium between dream and reality; the place where fantasy and earthy things are metamorphosed into a work of art; the hour when faith in the future becomes knowledge of the past; to lay down one's powers for others in need; to shake off the old ordeal and get ready for the new; to question, knowing that never can the full answer be found; to accept uncertainties quietly, even our incomplete knowledge of God: this is what man's journey is about, I think.

Lillian Smith : *The Journey*

THE PROUD KING

Jacob Glatstein

When the proud king rode into the enemy's city, his red beard flamed in the rising sun, like the gleaming swords of his retinue. And when the proud king saw that Death held the city in his embrace, and that all the bricks of the houses were dead, and the slightest breeze could blow the buildings into dust, he laughed. And he turned his thick-set head to view his retainers who jadedly and dully dragged after themselves an exhausted victory.

And the king ordered the youngest males of the city to come to meet him with bread and salt. Presently ten old men with long gray beards approached the king and fell upon their knees: "Proud king, we are the youngest males of the city, and we have no bread, for there has been a bread famine since all the last twelvemonth. Our lean arms, our dried palates bear witness thereto; a pinch of salt we have brought — only a pinch of salt we have brought."

Again the proud king looked back upon his fellows, who could scarcely stand upon their feet, dragging along an exhausted victory. The king ordered: "Let your most beautiful women come to meet my warriors — let them strew flowers before the advent of our victory." In weeping array the young women with grey heads walked barefoot and strewed withered petals. And the first four women bowed to the proud king and spake thus: "The breath of Death has dried up all our springs — like the roots of our hair — and our skies turned unto stone. How could we quench the flowers' thirst with empty jugs?" And the oldest male rose from the ground and spake thus: "Proud King, do not heed my bent head and my unsure tread. It is age that put a staff into my hand and bent my head. Age will also cover thy haughty head with ashes and command thee go in beggarly fashion." The proud king realized that presently his ire ought to flame forth like his ruddy beard. But he was not aroused. His eyes merely glanced over the withered petals that the young women had strewn before the advance of his victory.

And one of the young women tore off the rags from her. Her nudity wept as she spake thus: "Proud King, behold! my limbs that knew of man now hang in shame, for the yearning within me for the father of my child consumed all my femininity. So may the womb of thy wife be barren forever." Once more the proud king understood that he ought to unleash his rage like a savage young ox. But he did not. His eyes kept roaming over the withered petals which the young women scattered before the tread of his victory.

A sinister fear enveloped all the houses. Frightened children called their mothers through the casements. From the churches there came the weeping of the pious pews for the young fathers of the city. The blind dozing belfry ringer awoke, his parchmentlike hands beseeching the bells as usual to toll forth the approaching vesper hour, but the mute tongue of the bell rang out a death knell — a death knell.

The sun had shrunk. A torrent came on. The rain drenched alike the heads of the allies and the heads of the enemy. The ten old men turned their backs upon the king and started for the church. And the haughty king still saw how in weeping array the young women with grey heads walked barefoot and strewed withered petals before the advance of his victory.

KUBLA KHAN; OR, A VISION IN A DREAM

Samuel Taylor Coleridge

In Xanadu did Kubla Khan
A stately pleasure-dome decree:
Where Alph, the sacred river, ran
Through caverns measureless to man
　　Down to a sunless sea.
So twice five miles of fertile ground
With walls and towers were girdled round:
And there were garden bright with sinuous rills,
Where blossomed many an incense-bearing tree;
And here were forests ancient as the hills,
Enfolding sunny spots of greenery.

But oh! that deep romantic chasm which slanted
Down the green hill athwart a cedarn cover!
A savage place! as holy and enchanted
As e'er beneath a waning moon was haunted
By woman wailing for her demon-lover!
And from this chasm, with ceaseless turmoil seething,
As if this earth in fast thick pants were breathing,
A mighty fountain momently was forced:
Amid whose swift half-intermitted burst
Huge fragments vaulted like rebounding hail,
Or chaffy grain beneath the thresher's flail:
And 'mid these dancing rocks at once and ever
It flung up momently the sacred river.
Five miles meandering with a mazy motion
Through wood and dale the sacred river ran,
Then reached the caverns measureless to man,
And sank in tumult to a lifeless ocean:
And 'mid this tumult Kubla heard from far
Ancestral voices prophesying war!

　　The shadow of the dome of pleasure
　　Floated midway on the waves;
　　Where was heard the mingled measure
　　From the fountain and the caves.
It was a miracle of rare device,
A sunny pleasure-dome with caves of ice!

　　A damsel with a dulcimer
　　In a vision once I saw:
　　It was an Abyssinian maid,
　　And on her dulcimer she played,
　　Singing of Mount Abora.
　　Could I revive within me
　　Her symphony and song,
　　To such a deep delight 'twould win me,
That with music loud and long,
I would build that dome in air,
That sunny dome! those caves of ice!
And all who heard should see them there,
And all should cry, Beware! Beware!
His flashing eyes, his floating hair!
Weave a circle round him thrice,
And close your eyes with holy dread,
For he on honey-dew hath fed,
And drunk the milk of Paradise.

THE MAN IN BRADFORD

Robert J. Pickles

He walks the city streets
awaiting a message
from the
Lord.
Open sandals and a brown robe
tied in the middle
by a knotted
cord.

He may be thirty-two;
What's that to you?

He stands and smiles,
blue eyes wide, at
passers-by.
Is that the light of truth
or madness
in his
eye?

And I hear the soft
but persistent cry:

crucify, crucify.

from PEARL

Anonymous

What John the Apostle once could see
I saw: a city of great renown,
Jerusalem, new-made royally
as though from heaven coming down.
Golden it burned, that bright city
that gleamed like glass, burnished gold-brown,
with noble gems ranged skilfully,
with twelve bantels well fastened down
on twelve foundations, in a rich crown.
Like a different jewel each storey shone.
He splendidly pictured this same town
in his Apocalypse, the Apostle John.

We are beginning to understand, and for ever, that the only acceptable religion for man is the one that will teach him first of all to recognize love and passionately serve this universe of which he is the most important element.

Teilhard de Chardin : *The Phenomenon of Man*

Attempting to be more than Man we become less.

William Blake : *The Four Zoas*

God also likes to play hide-and-seek, but because there is nothing outside God, he has no one but himself to play with. But he gets over this difficulty by pretending that he is not himself. This is his way of hiding from himself. He pretends that he is you and I and all the people in the world, all the animals, all the plants, all the rocks, and all the stars. In this way he has strange and wonderful adventures, some of which are terrible and frightening. But these are just like bad dreams, for when he wakes up they will disappear.

Dunstan and Garlan : *Worlds in the Making*

Here he comes, stumbling down his ten thousand technological years – the fragmented man; a thing of bits and pieces cast upon the mudflats of the 20th Century by wayward tides and waves too high.

This is a mosaic that walks, wearing all his yesterdays like tattoos. Little, or nothing, in all his ancient heritage fits him for this moment. There is always something coming ashore, and he is doing so now. He strides into the spectrum as once the lonely horseman rode into the sunset of another time and place.

And no one knows what new adventures await him now.

Don Fabun : *Dynamics of Change*

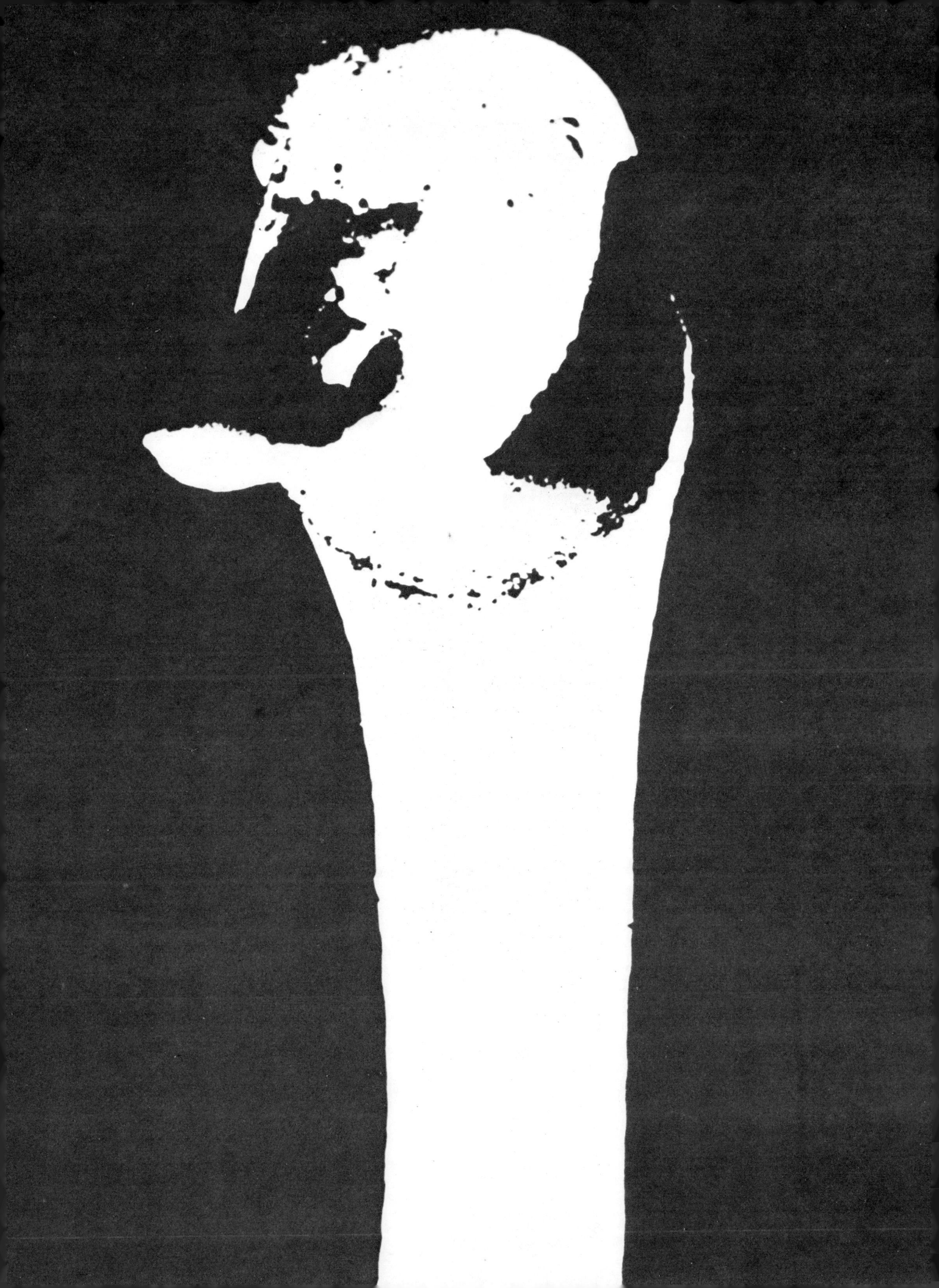

There is a new science appearing today. It is partly biology, partly anthropology, partly ethology. Because it is such a shifting mixture of parts, it is having a hard time defining itself as a separate discipline. As sciences go, it is rather beautiful: it gathers information, proposes theories, and offers insights, but so far it has produced no experts. Its proponents are learned human men; and they are generalists, not specialists.

>Robert Ardrey: *The Territorial Imperative*
>Desmond Morris: *The Naked Ape*
>Konrad Lorenz: *On Aggression*
>John Bleibtreu: *The Parable of the Beast*

What they offer together is a reminder of feeling as old as history, the reminder that we participate in the animal world just as we aspire above it. It does us well to recognize our place in the world of nature since over many centuries in the western world we have sought to rise above it, and to kill the beast in ourselves. St. Paul visualized beasts being cast into the outer darkness. The Book of Revelations foresaw a Beast appearing malevolently on the Day of Judgement. But these are very narrow visions of animal nature. Today, scientists and poets remind us that the darkness of beasts is not merely evil; it is also the natural sureness of living within nature, and acting out of intuition and the body's knowledge as well as the reason and the brain. The darkness of blood, the river of life, runs through
THE DARKNESS OF BEASTS.

THE HORSES

Edwin Muir

Barely a twelvemonth after
The seven days war that put the world to sleep,
Late in the evening the strange horses came.
By then we had made our covenant with silence,
But in the first few days it was so still
We listened to our breathing and were afraid.
On the second day
The radios failed; we turned the knobs; no answer.
On the third day a warship passed us, heading north,
Dead bodies piled on the deck. On the sixth day
A plane plunged over us into the sea. Thereafter
Nothing. The radios dumb;
And still they stand in corners of our kitchens,
And stand, perhaps, turned on, in a million rooms
All over the world. But now, if they should speak,
If on a sudden they should speak again,
If on the stroke of noon a voice should speak,
We would not listen, we would not let it bring
That old bad world that swallowed its children quick
At one great gulp. We would not have it again.
Sometimes we think of the nations lying asleep,
Curled blindly in impenetrable sorrow,
And then the thought confounds us with its strangeness.

The tractors lie about our fields; at evening
They look like dank sea-monsters couched and waiting.
We leave them where they are and let them rust:
'They'll moulder away and be like other loam'.
We make our oxen drag our rusty ploughs,
Long laid aside. We have gone back
Far past our fathers' land.

And then, that evening
Late in the summer the strange horses came.
We heard a distant tapping on the road,
A deepening drumming; it stopped, went on again
And at the corner changed to hollow thunder.
We saw the heads
Like a wild wave charging and were afraid.
We had sold our horses in our fathers' time
To buy new tractors. Now they were strange to us
As fabulous steeds set on an ancient shield
Or illustrations in a book of knights.
We did not dare go near them. Yet they waited,
Stubborn and shy, as if they had been sent
By an old command to find our whereabouts
And that long-lost archaic companionship
In the first moment we had never a thought
That they were creatures to be owned and used.
Among them were some half-a-dozen colts
Dropped in some wilderness of the broken world,
Yet new as if they had come from their own Eden.
Since then they have pulled our ploughs and borne our loads,
But that free servitude still can pierce our hearts.
Our life is changed; their coming our beginning.

The apple tree never asks the beech how he shall grow;
nor the lion, the horse, how he shall take his prey.

William Blake : *Marriage of Heaven and Hell*

It is of dangerous consequence to represent to man how near he is the level of beasts without showing him at the same time his greatness. It is likewise dangerous to let him see his greatness without his meanness. It is more dangerous yet to leave him ignorant of either; but very beneficial that he should be made sensible of both.

Blaise Pascal : *Pensées*

THE LAST WOLF

Alastair W. Thomson

We killed at noon,
Where snow had withered from the yellow grass,
The last wolf in the hills.
Hounds circled in the wind, a horn
Blew to the crofts below.

The torn muzzle, the dark savaged fur,
Lay in the stillness like a trodden rug.
Whatever else, had gone
Out of the reach of axe or gun,
And had become
A black crag, or the wind.

We nailed the head
To a gnarled pear-tree by the wall;
Put up the guns, laid the axe by the wood-pile.
And under the rain, the melting spring,
It rotted slowly into bone;
White tusk of bone among the blossom
Of a warm spring, the land at peace.

Than such a blossom, nothing more.
Crops withered, udders dried;
The cobles found strange tides, but never fish,
And the wild berries only brought
The dry and dying land upon the tongue.

Now at the autumn's end
Black hail comes storming from the sea, beats down
The glens and valleys and the staving straths;
Wolf-weather, reiving snow.

PEFFERLAW (Staff) — For 90 minutes during a 20-mile chase on Lake Simcoe, two snowmobile operators yesterday chased and hit a small brush wolf with their machines 20 times.

The exhausted animal was finally trapped against a mound of snow. The snowmobilers then jumped their machines over the mound to land on the wolf, breaking its back.

The incident occurred about three miles from shore, about 1½ miles east of Duclos Point.

The snowmobile drivers applied for the $20 wolf bounty.

The Toronto Telegram

THE WOLVES

Allen Tate

There are wolves in the next room waiting
With heads bent low, thrust out, breathing
At nothing in the dark; between them and me
A white door patched with light from the hall
Where it seems never (so still is the house)
A man has walked from the front door to the stair.
It has all been forever. Beasts claw the floor.
I have brooded on angels and arch fiends
But no man has ever sat where the next room's
Crowded with wolves, and for the honour of man
I affirm that never have I before. Now while
I have looked for the evening star at a cold window
And whistled when Arcturus split his light,
I've heard the wolves scuffle, and said: So this
Is man; so — what better conclusion is there —
The day will not follow night, and the heart
Of man has a little dignity, but less patience
Than a wolf's, and a duller sense that cannot
Smell its own mortality. (This and other
Meditations will be suited to other times
After dog silence howls his epitaph.)
Now remember courage, go to the door,
Open it and see whether coiled on the bed
Or cringing by the wall, a savage beast
Maybe with golden hair, with deep eyes
Like a bearded spider on a sunlit floor
Will snarl — and man can never be alone.

TRAVELLING THROUGH THE DARK

William Stafford

Travelling through the dark I found a deer
dead on the edge of the Wilson River road.
It is usually best to roll them into the canyon:
that road is narrow; to swerve might make more dead.

By glow of the tail-light I stumbled back of the car
and stood by the heap, a doe, a recent killing;
she had stiffened already, almost cold.
I dragged her off; she was large in the belly.

My fingers touching her side brought me the reason –
her side was warm; her fawn lay there waiting,
alive, still never to be born.
Beside that mountain road I hesitated.

The car aimed ahead its lowered parking lights;
under the hood purred the steady engine.
I stood in the glare of the warm exhaust turning red;
around our group I could hear the wilderness listen.

I thought hard for us all – my only swerving –
then pushed her over the edge into the river.

TAKE ONE HOME FOR THE KIDDIES

Philip Larkin

On shallow straw, in shadeless glass,
Huddled by empty bowls, they sleep:
No dark, no dam, no earth, no grass –
Mam, get us one of them to keep.

Living toys are something novel,
But it soon wears off somehow.
Fetch the shoebox, fetch the shovel –
Mam, we're playing funerals now.

Who is violent?
Man, and only man, is violent

  Every other species of God's creation takes its chance in the membrane-to-membrane, eye-to-eye, fang-to-claw dance of survival.

  Man is the only species who violates by distance weaponry.

Countdown

THE KILLER

Judith Wright

The day was clear as fire,
the birds sang frail as glass,
when thirsty I came to the creek
and fell by its side in the grass.

My breast on the bright moss
and shower-embroidered weeds,
my lips to the live water,
I saw him turn in the reeds.

Black horror sprang from the dark
in a violent birth,
and through its cloth of grass
I felt the clutch of earth.

O beat him into the ground.
O strike him till he dies,
or else your life itself
drains through those colourless eyes.

I struck again and again.
Slender in black and red
he lies, and his icy glance
turns outward, clear and dead.

But nimble my enemy
as water is, or wind.
He has slipped from his death aside
and vanished into my mind.

He has vanished whence he came,
my nimble enemy;
and the ants come out to the snake
and drink at his shallow eye.

MOUNTAIN LION

D. H. Lawrence

Climbing through the January snow, into the Lobo Canyon
Dark grow the spruce-trees, blue is the balsam, water sounds
    still unfrozen, and the trail is still evident.

Men!
Two men!
Men!   The only animal in the world to fear!

They hesitate.
We hesitate.
They have a gun.
We have no gun.

Then we all advance, to meet.

Two Mexicans, strangers, emerging out of the dark and snow
    and inwardness of the Lobo valley.
What are they doing here on this vanishing trail?

What is he carrying?
Something yellow.
A deer?

Qué tiene, amigo?
León –

He smiles, foolishly, as if he were caught doing wrong.
And we smile, foolishly, as if we didn't know.
He is quite gentle and dark-faced.

It is a mountain lion,
A long, long slim cat, yellow like a lioness,
Dead.

He trapped her this morning, he says, smiling foolishly.

RIVERDALE LION

John Robert Colombo

Bound lion, almost blind from meeting their gaze and popcorn,
    the Saturday kids love you. It is their parents
who would paint your mane with polkadots to match
    their California shirts
and would trim your nails for tieclips.

Your few roars delight them. But they wish you would
    quicken your pace
and not disappear so often into your artificial cave
for there they think you partake of secret joys and race
through the jungle-green lair of memory
under an African sun as gold as your mane.

But you fool them. You merely suffer the heat and scatter the flies
with your tail. You never saw Africa.
The sign does not tell them that you were born here, in captivity,
That you are as much a Canadian as they are.

Lift up her face,
Her round, bright face, bright as frost.
Her round, fine-fashioned head, with two dead ears;
And stripes in the brilliant frost of her face, sharp,
fine dark rays,
Beautiful dead eyes.

Hermoso es!

They go out towards the open;
We go on into the gloom of Lobo.
And above the trees I found her lair,
A hole in the blood-orange brilliant rocks that stick up,
    a little cave.
And bones, and twigs, and a perilous ascent.

So, she will never leap up that way again, with yellow flash
    of a mountain lion's long shoot!
And her bright striped frost-face will never watch any more,
    out of the shadow of the cave in the blood-orange rock.
Above the trees of the Lobo dark valley-mouth!

Instead, I look out.
And out to the dim of the desert, like a dream, never real;
To the snow of the Sangre de Cristo mountains, the ice of
    the mountains of Picoris,
And near across at the opposite steep of snow, green trees
    motionless standing in snow, like a Christmas toy.

And I think in this empty world there was room for me and a
    mountain lion.
And I think in the world beyond, how easily we might spare a
    million or two of humans
And never miss them.
Yet what a gap in the world, the missing white frost-face
of that slim yellow mountain lion.
                        Lobo

AU JARDIN DES PLANTES

John Wain

The gorilla lay on his back,
One hand cupped under his head,
Like a man.
Like a labouring man tired with work,
A strong man with his strength burnt away
In the toil of earning a living.

Only of course he was not tired out with work,
Merely with boredom; his terrible strength
All burnt away by prodigal idleness.

A thousand days, and then a thousand days,
Idleness licked away his beautiful strength
He having no need to earn a living.

It was all laid on, free of charge.
We maintained him, not for doing anything,
But for being what he was.

And so that Sunday morning he lay on his back,
Like a man, like a worn-out man,
One hand cupped under his terrible hard head.

Like a man, like a man,
One of those we maintain, not for doing anything,
But for being what they are.

A thousand days, and then a thousand days,
With everything laid on, free of charge,
They cup their heads in prodigal idleness.

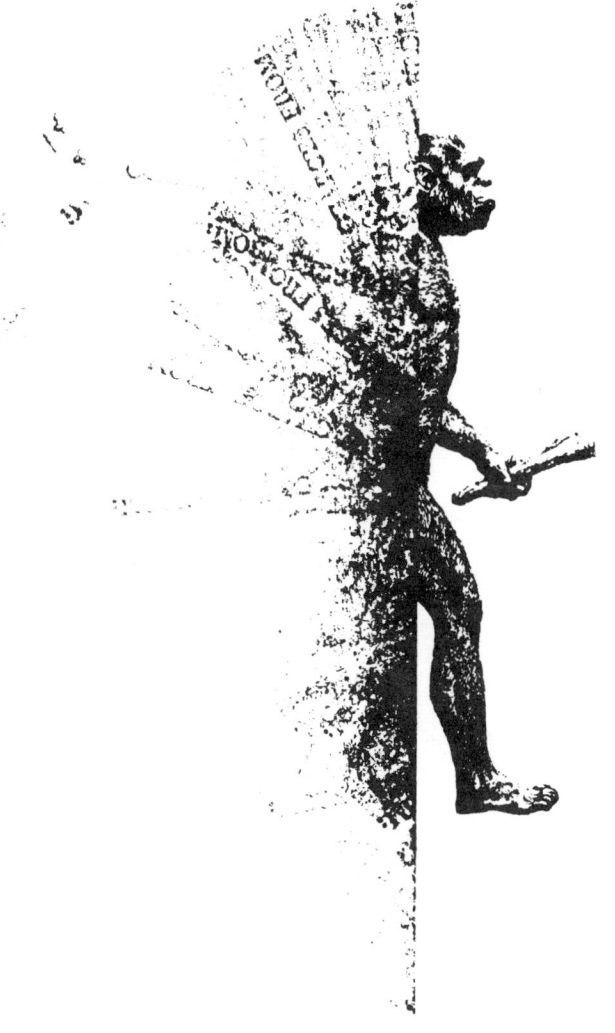

MAN AND BEAST

Clifford Dyment

Hugging the ground by the lilac tree,
With shadows in conspiracy,

The black cat from the house next door
Waits with death in each bared claw

For the tender unwary bird
That all the summer I have heard

In the orchard singing. I hate
The cat that is its savage fate,

And choose a stone with which to send
Slayer, not victim, to its end.

I look to where the black cat lies,
But drop my stone, seeing its eyes –

Who is it sins now, those eyes say,
You the hunter, or I the prey?

HOCKEY PLAYERS

Alfred Purdy

What they worry about most is injuries
        broken arms and legs and
fractured skulls opening so doctors
can see such bloody beautiful things
almost not quite happening in the bone rooms
        as they happen outside –

And the referee?
        He's right there on the ice
not out of sight among the roaring blue gods
of a game played for passionate businessmen
and a nation of television agnostics
who never agree with the referee and applaud
when he falls flat on his face –

        On a breakaway
the centre man carrying the puck
his wings trailing a little
        on both sides why
I've seen the aching glory of a resurrection
        in their eyes
        if they score
but crucifixion's agony to lose
– the game?

        We sit up there in the blues
bored and sleepy and suddenly three men
break down the ice in roaring feverish speed and
we stand up in our seats with such a rapid pouring
of delight exploding out of self to join them why
theirs and our orgasm is the rocket stipent
for skating thru the smoky end boards out
of sight and climbing up the appalachian highlands
and racing breast to breast across laurentian barrens
over hudson's diamond bay and down the treeless
        tundra where
auroras are tubercular and awesome and
stopping isn't feasible or possible or lawful
but we have to and we have to
        laugh because we must and
stop to look at self and one another but
        our opponent's never geography
          or distance why
        it's men
         –just men?

And how do the players feel about it
this combination of ballet and murder?
For years a Canadian specific
to salve the anguish of inferiority
by being good at something the Americans aren't –
And what's the essence of a game like this
which takes a ten year fragment of a man's life
replaced with love that lodges in his brain
        and takes the place of reason?
Besides the fear of injuries
is it the difficulty of ever really overtaking
a hard black rubber disc?
Is it the impatient coach who insists on winning?
Sportswriters friendly but sometimes treacherous?
– And the worrying wives wanting you to quit and
your aching body stretched on the rubbing table
thinking of money in owner's pocket that might be in yours
the butt-slapping camaraderie and the self indulgence
of allowing yourself to be a hero and knowing
everything ends in a pot-belly –
Out on the ice can all these things be forgotten
in swift and skilled delight of speed?
– roaring out the endboards out the city
streets and high up where laconic winds
whisper litanies for a fevered hockey player –
Or racing breast to breast and never stopping
over rooftops of the world and all together
sing the song of winning all together
sing the song of money all together ...

        (and out in the suburbs
there's the six year old kid
whose reflexes were all wrong
who always fell down and hurt himself and cried
and never learned to skate
        with his friends) –

DOG

Lawrence Ferlinghetti

The dog trots freely in the street
and sees reality
and the things he sees
are bigger than himself
and the things he sees
are his reality
Drunks in doorways
Moons on trees
The dog trots freely thru the street
and the things he sees
are smaller than himself
Fish on newsprint
Ants in holes
Chickens in Chinatown windows
their heads a block away
The dog trots freely in the street
and the things he smells
smell something like himself
The dog trots freely in the street
past puddles and babies
cats and cigars
poolrooms and policemen
He doesn't hate cops
He merely has no use for them
and he goes past them
and past the dead cows hung up whole
in front of the San Francisco Meat Market
He would rather eat a tender cow
than a tough policeman
though either might do
And he goes past the Romeo Ravioli Factory
and past Coit's Tower
and past Congressman Doyle
He's afraid of Coit's Tower
but he's not afraid of Congressman Doyle
although what he hears is very discouraging
very depressing
very absurd
to a sad young dog like himself
to a serious dog like himself
But he has his own free world to live in
His own fleas to eat
He will not be muzzled
Congressman Doyle is just another
fire hydrant
to him

The dog trots freely in the street
and has his own dog's life to live
and to think about
and to reflect upon
touching and tasting and testing everything
investigating everything
without benefit of perjury
a real realist
with a real tale to tell
and a real tail to tell it with
a real live
   barking
     democratic dog
engaged in real
   free enterprise
with something to say
   about ontology
something to say
   about reality
     and how to see it
      and how to hear it
with his head cocked sideways
   at streetcorners
as if he is just about to have
   his picture taken
     for Victor Records
   listening for
     His Master's Voice
  and looking
   like a living questionmark
     into the
     great gramaphone
     of puzzling existence
with its wondrous hollow horn
  which always seems
  just about to spout forth
    some Victorious answer
     to everything

THE RAT OF TOK-CHONG

Bruton Conners

At Tok-Chong, a rat,
Cropping dust on the highway,
Saw the assassin
And the stone smashed him sideways.
As the lorry started,
He hid in the space
Of the hub and the tyre.
He spun for five seconds
Inside the wheel
And as he dripped out,
The second rock broke him.
He entered and spun
Four times and dropped out,
Then, as the stoning continued,
Small, dusty, insane
He died.

SLUGS

Anon.

Slugs, soft upon damp
carpets of rich food
Silvery, flaccid, they
consider lewd the use of eyes.

THE EAGLE

Alfred, Lord Tennyson

He clasps the crag with crooked hands;
Close to the sun in lonely lands,
Ringed with the azure world, he stands.

The wrinkled sea beneath him crawls;
He watches from his mountain walls,
And like a thunderbolt he falls.

WOODPECKER

Anon.

Above the cherry blossoms,
the woodpecker flies,
looking for dead
             wood.

BUTTERFLIES

Chu Miao Tuan

The blossoms fall like snowflakes
On the cool, deep, dark-green moss,
They lie in white-heaped fragrant drifts
Before the courtyard gates.

The butterflies, not knowing
That the days of spring are done,
Still pursue the flying petals
Across the garden wall.

THE BEAR ON THE DELHI ROAD

Earle Birney

Unreal   tall as a myth
by the road the Himalayan bear
is beating the brilliant air
with his crooked arms
About him two men bare
spindly as locusts   leap

One pulls on a ring
in the great soft nose   His mate
flicks   flicks with a stick
up at the rolling eyes

They have not led him here
down from the fabulous hills
to this bald alien plain
and the clamorous world   to kill
but simply to teach him to dance

They are peaceful both   these spare
men of Kashmir and the bear
alive is their living   too
If   far on the Delhi way
around him galvanic they dance
it is merely to wear   wear
from his shaggy body the tranced
wish forever to stay
only an ambling bear
four-footed in berries

It is no more joyous for them
in this hot dust to prance
out of reach of the praying claws
sharpened to paw for ants
in the shadows of deodars
It is not easy to free
myth from reality
or rear this fellow up
to lurch   lurch with them
in the tranced dancing of men

A sentimental misanthropist coined the often cited aphorism "The more I see of human beings, the more I like animals." I maintain the contrary: only the person who knows animals, including the highest and most nearly related to ourselves, and who has gained insight into evolution, will be able to apprehend the unique position of man. We are the highest achievement reached so far by the great constructors of evolution. We are their "latest" but certainly not their last word. The scientist must not regard anything as absolute, not even the laws of pure reason. He must remain aware of the great fact, discovered by Heraclitus, that nothing whatever really remains the same even for one moment but that everything is perpetually changing. To regard man, the most ephemeral and rapidly evolving of all species, as the final and unsurpassable achievement of creation, especially at his present-day particularly dangerous and disagreeable stage of development, is certainly the most arrogant and dangerous of all untenable doctrines. If I thought of man as the final image of God, I should not know what to think of God. But when I consider that our ancestors, at a time fairly recent in relation to the earth's history, were perfectly ordinary apes, closely related to chimpanzees, I see a glimmer of hope. It does not require considerable optimism to assume that from us human beings something better and higher may evolve. Far from seeing in man the irrevocable and unsurpassable image of God, I assert – more modestly and, I believe, in greater awe of the Creation and its infinite possibilities – that the long-sought missing link between animals and the really humane being is ourselves!

Konrad Lorenz : *On Aggression*

THE ORANGE BEARS

Kenneth Patchen

The orange bears with soft friendly eyes
Who played with me when I was ten,
Christ, before I left home they'd had
Their paws smashed in rolls, their backs
Seared by hot slag, their soft trusting
Bellies kicked in, their tongues ripped
Out, and I went down through the woods
To the smelly crick with Whitman
In the Haldeman Julius edition,
And I just sat there worrying my thumbnail
Into the cover – What did he know about
Orange bears with their coats all strunk up with soft coal
And the National Guard coming over
From Wheeling to stand in front of the millgates
With drawn bayonets jeering at the strikers?
I remember you could put daisies
On the windowsill at night and in
The morning they'd be so covered with soot
You couldn't tell what they were anymore.

A hell of a fat chance my orange bears had!

Since man is a primate with weaker instincts than the reindeer, the horse, and the goat, he may be a readier subject for domestication. We cannot be sure. Human slavery has represented man's only persistent attempt to tame his fellow man. The slave as a rule, however, was cheaper to buy or to capture than to breed; and so we cannot interpret the collapse of slavery as the failure of controlled human breeding. We and our greater philosophers must grant, I believe, that the masters of a universal society with the aid of a captive science might just possibly succeed in producing, over a long enough period, a lasting answer to the problem of our animal nature: a universal slave inherently obedient to other people's reason.

Whether through sentimental attachment or rational choice, I find myself moved to prefer the wild creatures among whom I was born to the more literal *Homo sapiens* that science and tyranny might unite to produce. I may in my preference be a victim of a new self-delusion, and be looking at human affairs through another transparent curtain. But I find that I cannot disbelieve in nature. I cannot but believe in the pure wild gene, in natural selection as opposed to human, and in the strength and balance of our natural endowment as sufficient foundation for our species' ambitions.

Robert Ardrey : *African Genesis*

ELEPHANTS

John Newlove

Elephants

aren't any more important
than insects

but I'm on the side
of elephants

unless one of them tries
to crawl up my leg

Linnaeus named us Homo sapiens, stressing through that choice of appellation, all the arrogance and vanity of eighteenth-century scientific certainties. In the two hundred years ensuing between his time and ours, these certainties and vanities have become blunted and muted; we no longer see ourselves as belonging to one order of living being as separate from any other order of living being. We are all interconnected by the fact of existence, the fact of life. And this fact of life ties us irrevocably into the past as determining great parts of the present.

John Bleibtreu: *The Parable of the Beast*

Think of it: when we have too many people, we have to lessen the number. One way is to keep some from being born. We already do that.

Another way is to get rid of some of those who are already born. We have to learn that now. Wars and famine and disease and accident have always been sufficient. But now that we are better at keeping ourselves alive, it looks as though we will have to get better at killing. Give a little extra effort to get a little extra space.

Who better to give than those who are young, hale and hearty – and who administer power, of course.

Who better to receive than those who are old, infirm or sick.

BY THE YEAR 2000: EUTHANASIA.

That is what being old might mean.
In the year 2000, how old will you be?
How about you?

CHILDHOOD

Frances Cornford

I used to think that grown-up people chose
To have stiff backs and wrinkles round their nose,
And veins like small fat snakes on either hand,
On purpose to be grand.
Till through the bannisters I watched one day
My great-aunt Etty's friend who was going away,
And how her onyx beads had come unstrung.
I saw her grope to find them as they rolled;
And then I knew that she was helplessly old,
As I was helplessly young.

THE FROST

Tzu Yeh

Young man,
Seize every minute
Of your time.
The days fly by;
Ere long you too
Will grow old.

If you believe me not,
See there, in the courtyard,
How the frost
Glitters white and cold and cruel
On the grass
That once was green.

AN OLD MAN'S LARK

Donald Jones

From the fine nursing home
unnoticed one afternoon
with saved-up spending money
from his children far away

he bolted across the lawn,
caught a streetcar downtown,
had two cheeseburgers, a malt,
and watched a double feature.

His money all gone, he spent
the summer night on a park bench,
was found there the next morning
by his helpers young and hurt.

TO A POOR OLD WOMAN

William Carlos Williams

munching a plum on
the street a paper bag
of them in her hand

They taste good to her
They taste good
to her. They taste
good to her

You can see it by
the way she gives herself
to the one half
sucked out in her hand

Comforted
a solace of ripe plums
seeming to fill the air
They taste good to her

ANCIENT MUSIC

Ezra Pound

Winter is icummen in,
Lhude sing Goddamm,
Raineth drop and staineth slop,
And how the wind doth ramm!
        Sing: Goddamm.
Skiddeth bus and sloppeth us,
An ague hath my ham.
Freezeth river, turneth liver,
        Damn you, sing: Goddamm.
Goddamm, Goddamm, 'tis why I am, Goddamm,
        So 'gainst the winter's balm,
Sing goddamm, damm, sing Goddamm,
Sing goddamm, sing goddamm, DAMM.

O Gilgamesh, this was the meaning of your dream. You were given the kingship, such was your destiny, everlasting life was not your destiny. Because of this do not be sad at heart, do not be grieved or oppressed; he has given you power to bind and to loose, to be the darkness and the light of mankind. He has given unexampled supremacy over the people, in victory in battle from which no fugitive returns, in forays and assaults from which there is no going back. But do not abuse this power, deal justly with your servants in the palace, deal justly before the face of the Sun.

    N. K. Sandars, trs. : *The Epic of Gilgamesh*

A MOMENT OF RESPECT

Edwin Brock

Two things I remember about my grandfather:
his threadbare trousers, and the way he adjusted
his half-hunter watch two minutes every day.

When I asked him why he needed to know the time so
exactly, he said a business man could lose a fortune
by being two minutes late for an appointment.

When he died he left two meerschaum pipes
and a golden sovereign on a chain. Somebody
threw the meerschaum pipes away, and
there was an argument about the sovereign.

On the day of his burial the church clock chimed
as he was lowered down into the clay, and all
the family advanced their watches by two minutes.

The older adult is not, then, a prisoner of time, nor does he feel that it is running out on him. He makes no effort to appear younger than he is. The minutes, hours, and days simply pass, filled up with a variety of activities which are performed as the need to do them arises. Time does not drag and it does not threaten; it is there to be used but it does not stretch emptily before the older person. He works at what he can do or he is of service to those whom he can help, and when he dies he can hope that his family will say of him that his last years were no more burden to himself than to others.

    Robert J. Smith : *"Cultural Differences and the Concept of Time"*

HEIRLOOM

A. M. Klein

My father bequeathed me no wide estates;
No keys and ledgers were my heritage;
Only some holy books with *yahrzeit* dates
Writ mournfully upon a blank front page –

Books of the Baal Shem Tov, and of his wonders;
Pamphlets upon the devil and his crew;
Prayers against road demons, witches, thunders;
And sundry other tomes for a good Jew.

Beautiful: Though no pictures on them save
The scorpion crawling on a printed track;
The Virgin floating on a scriptural wave,
Square letters twinkling in the Zodiac.

The snuff left on this page, now brown and old,
The tallow stains of midnight liturgy –
These are my coat of arms, and these unfold
My noble lineage, my proud ancestry!

And my tears, too, have stained this heirloomed ground,
When reading in these treatises some weird
Miracle, I turned a leaf and found
A white hair fallen from my father's beard.

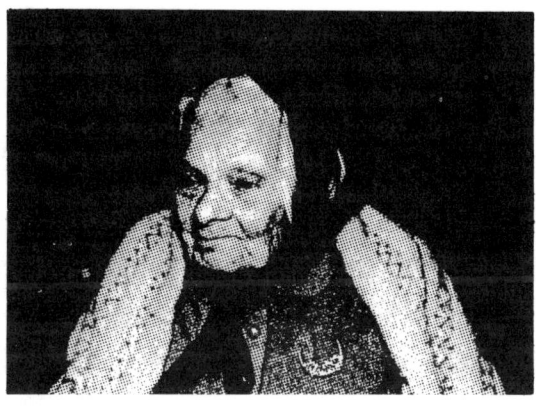

AN OLD MAN'S WINTER NIGHT

Robert Frost

All out of doors looked darkly in at him
Through the thin frost, almost in separate stars,
That gathers on the pane in empty rooms.
What kept his eyes from giving back the gaze
Was the lamp tilted near them in his hand.
What kept him from remembering the need
That brought him to that creaking room was age,
He stood with barrels round him – at a loss.
And having scared the cellar under him
In clomping off; – and scared the outer night,
Which has its sounds, familiar, like the roar
Of trees and crack of branches, common things,
But nothing so like beating on a box.

A light he was to no one but himself
Where now he sat, concerned with he knew what,
A quiet light, and then not even that.
He consigned to the moon, such as she was,
So late-arising, to the broken moon
As better than the sun in any case
For such a charge, his snow upon the roof,
His icicles along the wall to keep;
And slept. The log that shifted with a jolt
Once in the stove, disturbed him and he shifted,
And eased his heavy breathing, but still slept.
One aged man – one man – can't keep a house,
A farm, a countryside, or if he can,
It's thus he does it of a winter night.

CRAZY JANE TALKS WITH THE BISHOP

William Butler Yeats

I met the Bishop on the road
And much said he and I.
"Those breasts are flat and fallen now,
Those veins must soon be dry;
Live in a heavenly mansion,
Not in some foul sty."

"Fair and foul are near of kin,
And fair needs foul," I cried.
"My friends are gone, but that's a truth
Nor grave nor bed denied,
Learned in bodily lowliness
And in the heart's pride.

"A woman can be proud and stiff
When on love intent;
But Love has pitched his mansion in
The place of excrement;
For nothing can be sole or whole
That has not been rent."

... The vitality of an individual diminishes as he walks and climbs through life, which is exactly what he does in the Andes. With every step he takes, he leaves behind little particles of his earth supply, and when this supply is finally used up, death follows.

It is the belief of these people that human existence unfolds vigorously until the middle year or, as they say, "the twelve o'clock of life." ... Fatigue is great in the old man because the path which he walked, labored, and climbed has eaten his life away.

Anon.

THE REBEL
Mari Evans
When I
die
I'm sure
I will have a
Big Funeral ...
Curiosity
seekers ...
coming to see
if I
am really
dead ...
or just
trying to make
Trouble. ...

GROWING OLD

Matthew Arnold

What is it to grow old?
Is it to lose the glory of the form,
The luster of the eye?
Is it for beauty to forego her wreath?
– Yes, but not this alone.

Is it to feel our strength –
Not our bloom only, but our strength – decay?
Is it to feel each limb
Grow stiffer, every function less exact,
Each nerve more loosely strung?

Yes, this, and more; but not
Ah, 'tis not what in youth we dreamed 'twould be!
'Tis not to have our life
Mellowed and softened as with sunset glow,
A golden day's decline.

'Tis not to see the world
As from a height, with rapt prophetic eyes,
And heart profoundly stirred;
And weep, and feel the fullness of the past,
The years that are not more.

It is to spend long days
And not once feel that we were ever young;
It is to add, immured
In the hot prison of the present, month
To month with weary pain.

It is to suffer this,
And feel but half, and feebly, what we feel.
Deep in our hidden heart
Festers the dull remembrance of a change,
But no emotion – none.

It is – last stage of all –
When we are frozen up within, and quite
The phantom of ourselves,
To hear the world applaud the hollow ghost
Which blamed the living man.

DO NOT GO GENTLE INTO THAT GOOD NIGHT

Dylan Thomas

Do not go gentle into that good night,
Old age should burn and rave at close of day;
Rage, rage against the dying of the light.

Though wise men at their end know dark is right,
Because their words have forked no lightning they
Do not go gentle into that good night.

Good men, the last wave by, crying how bright
Their frail deeds might have danced in a green bay,
Rage, rage against the dying of the light.

Wild men who caught and sang the sun in flight,
And learn, too late, they grieved it on its way,
Do not go gentle into that good night.

Grave men, near death, who see with blinding sight
Blind eyes could blaze like meteors and be gay,
Rage, rage against the dying of the light.

And you, my father, there on the sad height,
Curse, bless, me now with your fierce tears, I pray.
Do not go gentle into that good night.
Rage, rage against the dying of the light.

OLD ALEX

Alfred Purdy

"85 years old, that miserable alcoholic
old bastard is never gonna die" the man said
where he got bed and board. But he did.
I'll say this about Alex' immortality tho:
if they dig him up in a thousand years
and push a spigot into his belly why
his fierce cackle'll drive a nail in silence,
his laugh split cordwood and trees kow-tow
like green butlers, the staggering world
get drunk and all the ghouls go scared –

So you say: was I fond of him?
No – not exactly anyhow. Once
he told his sons and daughters to stay away,
and then vomited on their memory. It'd be
like liking toadstools or a gun pointing at you –

He sat home three weeks drinking whiskey,
singing harsh songs and quoting verse and chapter
from the Bible: his mean and privileged piety
dying slowly: they rolled him onto a stretcher
like an old pig and prettied him with cosmetics,
sucked his blood out with a machine and
dumped him into the ground like garbage –

I don't mourn. Nobody does. Like mourning an ulcer.
Why commemorate disease in a poem then?
I don't know. But his hate was lovely,
given freely and without stint. His smallness
had the quality of making everyone else feel noble,
and thus fools. I search desperately
for good qualities and end up crawling
inside that decaying head and wattled throat
to scream obscenities like papal blessings,
knowing now and again I'm at least God –
Well, who remembers a small purple and yellow bruise long?
But when he was here he was a sunset!

The road of excess leads to the palace of wisdom.
In seed time learn, in harvest teach, in winter enjoy.
The cistern contains: the fountain overflows.
Drive your cart and your plow over the bones of the dead.
The fox provides for himself, but God provides for the lion.
Exuberance is Beauty.
Damn braces. Bless relaxes.

If the fool would persist in his folly he would become wise.
Prudence is a rich, ugly old maid courted by Incapacity.
Think in the morning. Act in the noon. Eat in the evening. Sleep in the night.
The pride of the peacock is the glory of God.
The lust of the goat is the bounty of God.
The nakedness of woman is the work of God.
The wrath of the lion is the wisdom of God.

William Blake : *Marriage of Heaven and Hell*

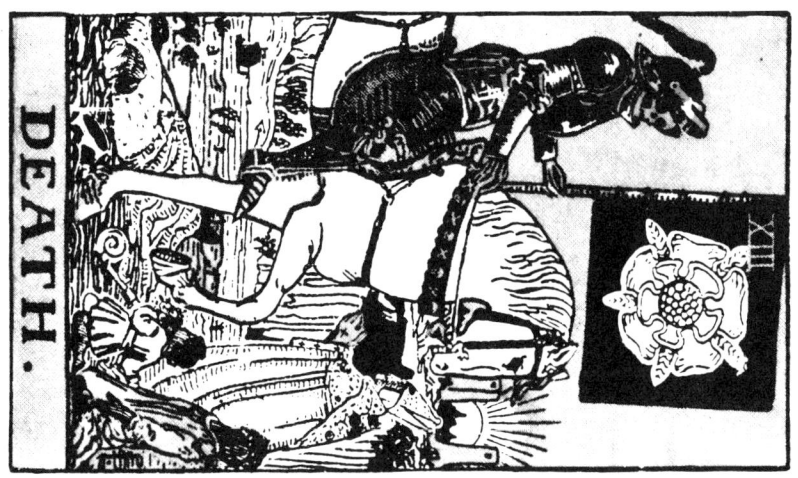

"And my youth returns, like the rains of Spring,
And my sons, like the wild geese flying;
And I lie and hear the meadow-lark sing
And have much content with my dying."

Stephen Vincent Benét : *"Ballad of William Sycamore"*

Horatio: O DAY AND NIGHT, BUT THIS IS WONDROUS STRANGE

All the hours of our waking and sleeping there is a beat of energy around us. Some of it our senses detect. Some of it, we suspect, is detected by something in us beyond or beneath or beside our senses. Some of it our tools and instruments tell us. Much of it we do not detect at all. We do not even know if it exists or not.

But we should know that where energy exists, whether radiant, kinetic, electrical or what have you, then the possibility of communication and art exists also. We should be prepared to see meaning where we find activity, whether in apparently random radio signals from the stars, or the graphic extensions of a concrete poem. Only if we are prepared, will we find it. As Hamlet said in reply to Horatio . . .

Hamlet: AND THEREFORE AS A STRANGER GIVE IT WELCOME

We can try welcoming the strange in these poems. They have within each of them something of a short circuit of the senses, and a puzzle to the reason.

Hamlet: THERE ARE MORE THINGS IN HEAVEN AND EARTH, HORATIO, THAN ARE DREAMT OF IN YOUR PHILOSOPHY.

SILENCE

Edgar Lee Masters

I have known the silence of the stars and of the sea,
And the silence of the city when it pauses,
And the silence of a man and a maid,
And the silence of the sick
When their eyes roam about the room.
And I ask: For the depths
Of what use is language?
A beast of the field moans a few times
When death takes its young.
And we are voiceless in the presence of realities —
We cannot speak.

A curious boy asks an old soldier
Sitting in front of the grocery store,
"How did you lose your leg?"
And the old soldier is struck with silence,
Or his mind flies away
Because he cannot concentrate it on Gettysburg.
It comes back jocosely
And he says, "A bear bit it off."
And the boy wonders, while the old soldier
Dumbly, feebly lives over
The flashes of guns, the thunder of cannon,
The shrieks of the slain,
And himself lying on the ground,
And the hospital surgeons, the knives,
And the long days in bed.
But if he could describe it all
He would be an artist.

> There is no system of philosophy to spin out. There are no ethical truths; there are just clarifications of particular ethical problems. Take advantage of these clarifications and work out your own existence. You are mistaken to think that anyone ever had the answers. There are no answers. Be brave and face up to it.
>
> Donald Kalish, Philosopher, U.C.L.A.

But if he were an artist there would be deeper wounds
Which he could not describe.
There is the silence of a great hatred,
And the silence of a great love,
And the silence of an embittered friendship.
There is the silence of a spiritual crisis,
Through which your soul, exquisitely tortured,
Comes with visions not to be uttered
Into a realm of higher life.
There is the silence of defeat.
There is the silence of those unjustly punished;
And the silence of the dying whose hand
Suddenly grips yours.
There is the silence between father and son,
When the father cannot explain his life,
Even though he be misunderstood for it.

There is the silence that comes between husband and wife.
There is the silence of those who have failed;
And the vast silence that covers
Broken nations and vanquished leaders.
There is the silence of Lincoln,
Thinking of the poverty of his youth.
And the silence of Napoleon
After Waterloo.
And the silence of Jeanne d'Arc
Saying amid the flames, "Blessed Jesus" —
Revealing in two words all sorrows, all hope.
And there is the silence of age,
Too full of wisdom for the tongue to utter it
In words intelligible to those who have not lived
The great range of life.

And there is the silence of the dead.
If we who are in life cannot speak
Of profound experiences,
Why do you marvel that the dead
Do not tell you of death?
Their silence shall be interpreted
As we approach them.

As Lorenz points out, aggressiveness can be taught. It is also intensified when it is exercised (and atrophies when it is not). When men began to settle in communities, they learned the irritations of being crowded. By then they had probably learned the use of weapons, originally for the purpose of killing game. And since they had already acquired at least a rudimentary speech, they could absorb from one another, and preach, animosity. With words, they could incite hatred against neighbouring tribes. A leader, coveting power or property, could, with propaganda, instill in his subjects admiration for warlike attitudes.

    Dunstan and Garlan : *Worlds in the Making*

A BLACK RABBIT DIES FOR ITS COUNTRY

Gavin Ewart

Born in the lab, I never saw the grass
or felt the direct touch of wind or sun
and if a rabbit's nature is to run
free on the earth, I missed it; though the glass
never let shot or eager predators pass

while I was against my mother's side;
something was waiting in the centrifuge
(the world's cage, although that cage is huge)
and separate I lived until I died –
watered and fed, I didn't fret, inside,

and all the time was waiting for the paste
scooped with a spatula from the metal rim,
and concentrate bacillus at the brim,
and lived the life of feeling and of taste.
I didn't know it. Knowing would be waste

in any case, and anthrax is the hard
stuff that knocks out the mice, the dogs, the men,
you haven't any chance at all and when
they've finished with you, you're down on a card.
How could I know, to be upon my guard

when they pushed my container into line
with the infected airstream? Breath is life;
though something there more deadly than the knife
cut into me, I was still feeling fine
and never guessed the next death would be mine

how many minutes later, lungs would choke
as feet beat out the seconds like a drum,
hands held me on the table, this was a sum
with the predicted ending of a joke.
Fighting I died, and no god even spoke.

PITY THIS BUSY MONSTER, MANUNKIND

e. e. cummings

pity this busy monster,manunkind,

not. Progress is a comfortable disease:
your victim(death and life safely beyond)

plays with the bigness of his littleness
– electrons deity one razorblade
into a mountainrange; lenses extend

unwish through curving wherewhen till unwish
returns on its unself.

          A world of made
is not a world of born – pity poor flesh

and trees,poor stars and stones,but never this
fine specimen of hypermagical

ultraomnipotence. We doctors know

a hopeless case if – listen;there's a hell
of a good universe next door;let's go

You are strapped to a table, shaped, ironically, like a cross, with a crown of electric sparks in place of thorns. You are touched on each side of the head with wires. Zap! Five cents' worth of electricity through the brain and you are jointly administered therapy and a punishment for your hostile go-to-hell behavior, on top of being put out of everyone's way for six hours to three days, depending on the individual. Even when you do regain consciousness you are in a state of disorientation for days. You are unable to think coherently. You can't recall things. Enough of these treatments and a man could turn out like Mr. Ellis you see over there against the wall. A drooling, pants-wetting idiot at thirty-five.

Ken Kesey : *One Flew Over the Cuckoo's Nest*

DEAD BEAT

David J. Lee

I'm lying in bed one day,
And this jerk
With tubes in his ears
sticks something cold on my chest,
And says something I can't hear.

It must be important,
Because soon people are washing me,
Like I got lice.
But I don't mind,
I'm too idle to wash myself.

And I say nothing
When my folks arrive,
And make with the tears.

But then they put me in this box:
It's comfortable,
But not exactly spacious.
And when they bang the lid on,
I'm worried, and I yell:
"Open the box"
But I can't,
And this guy upstairs says:
"How do you like the mystery prize?"
And I don't.

HAIKU: TWO FAMOUS JAPANESE

Buson

1 Going along the valley path,
 People are small:
 Ah, the young leaves!

2 How tiny the men,
 Going along the valley path,
 Among the green leaves!

I'D LIKE

Piet Hein

I'd like to know
what this whole show
is all about
before it's out.

MAKING SENSE

Piet Hein

Life makes sense,
and who could doubt it,
if we have
no doubt about it.

ICARUS ALLSORTS

Roger McGough

*"A meteorite is reported to have landed
in New England. No damage is said . . ."*

A littlebit of heaven fell
From out the sky one day
It landed in the ocean
Not so very far away
The General at the radar screen
Rubbed his hands with glee
And grinning pressed the button
That started World War Three.

From every corner of the earth
Bombs began to fly
There were even missile jams
No traffic lights in the sky
In the times it takes to blow your nose
The people fell, the mushrooms rose

"House!" cried the fatlady
As the bingohall moved to various parts
of the town

"Raus!" cried the German butcher
as his shop came tumbling down

Philip was in the countinghouse
Counting out his money
The Queen was in the parlour
Eating bread and honey
When through the window
Flew a bomb
And made them go all funny

(By the way if you're wondering
What happened to the maid
Well in this particular raid
She lost more than her nose
In fact she came to a close
Or so the story goes.)

In the time it takes to draw a breath
Or eat a toadstool, instant death.

The rich
Huddled outside the doors of their fallout shelters
Like drunken carolsingers

The poor
Clutching shattered televisions
And last week's editions of T.V. Times
(but the very last)

Civil defence volunteers
Withtheir tin hats in one hand
And their heads in the other

CND supporters
Theirban the bomb mojos beginning to rust
Have scrawled "I told you so" in the dust.

A littlebit of heaven fell
From out the sky one day
It landed in Vermont
North-Eastern U.S.A.
The general at the radar screen
He should have got the sack
But that wouldn't bring
Three thousand million, seven hundred,
    and sixty-eight people back,
Would it?

"What an optimistic animal man is!" said Rumfoord rosily. "Imagine expecting the species to last for ten million more years – as though people were as well-designed as turtles!" He shrugged. "Well – who knows – maybe human beings will last that long, just on the basis of pure cussedness. What's your guess?"

Kurt Vonnegut : *Sirens of Titan*

You may ask why God sometimes hides in the form of horrible people, or pretends to be people who suffer great disease and pain. Remember, first, that he isn't really doing this to anyone but himself. Remember, too, that in almost all the stories you enjoy there have to be bad people as well as good people, for the thrill of the tale is to find out how the good people will get the better of the bad. It's the same as when we play cards. At the beginning of the game we shuffle them all into a mess, which is like the bad things in the world, but the point of the game is to put the mess into good order, and the one who does it best is the winner. Then we shuffle the cards once more and play again, and so it goes with the world.

Dunstan and Garlan : *Worlds in the Making*

WARTY BLIGGENS THE TOAD

Don Marquis

i met a toad
the other day by the name
of warty bliggens
he was sitting under
a toadstool
feeling contented
he explained that when the cosmos
was created
that toadstool was especially
planned for his personal
shelter from sun and rain
thought out and prepared
for him

do not tell me
said warty bliggens
that there is not a purpose
in the universe
the thought is blasphemy

a little more
conversation revealed
that warty bliggens
considers himself to be
the center of the said
universe
the earth exists
to grow toadstools for him
to sit under
the sun to give him light
by day and the moon
and wheeling constellations
to make beautiful
the night for the sake of
warty bliggens

to what act of yours
do you impute
this interest on the part
of the creator
of the universe
i asked him
why is it that you
are so greatly favored

ask rather
said warty bliggens
what the universe
has done to deserve me
if i were a
human being i would
not laugh
too complacently
at poor warty bliggens
for similar
absurdities
have only too often
lodged in the crinkles
of the human cerebrum

archy

WORMS AND THE WIND

Carl Sandburg

Worms would rather be worms.
Ask a worm and he says, "Who knows what a worm knows?"
Worms go down and up and over and under.
Worms like tunnels.
When worms talk they talk about the worm world.
Worms like it in the dark.
Neither the sun nor the moon interests a worm.
Zigzag worms hate circle worms.
Curve worms never trust square worms.
Worms know what worms want.
Slide worms are suspicious of crawl worms.
One worm asks another, "How does your belly drag today?"
The shape of a crooked worm satisfies a crooked worm.
A straight worm says, "Why not be straight?"
Worms tired of crawling begin to slither.
Long worms slither farther than short worms.
Middle-sized worms say, "It is nice to be neither long nor short."
Old worms teach young worms to say,
   "Don't be sorry for me unless you have been a worm and lived in worm places and
     read worm books."
When worms go to war they dig in, come out and fight, dig in again, come out and fight
    again, dig in again, and so on.
Worms underground never hear the wind overground and sometimes they ask,
   "What is this wind we hear of?"

But it will be objected that, if there is no *idea* signified by the terms "soul," "spirit," and "substance," they are wholly insignificant, or have no meaning in them. I answer, those words do mean or signify a real thing – which is neither an idea nor like an idea, but that which perceives ideas, and wills, and reasons about them. What I am myself – that which I denote by the term *I* – is the same with what is meant by *soul* or *spiritual substance*. But if I should say that *I* was nothing, or that *I* was an idea, nothing could be more evidently absurd than either of these propositions. If it be said that this is only quarrelling at a word, and that, since the *immediate* significations of other names are by common consent called *ideas*, no reason can be assigned why that which is signified by the name *spirit* or *soul* may not partake in the same appellation. I answer – All the unthinking objects of the mind agree in that they are entirely passive, and their existence consists only in being perceived; whereas a soul or spirit is an active being, whose existence consists, not in being perceived, but in perceiving ideas and thinking.

    Bishop Berkeley : *Principles of Human Knowledge*

THE RHYTHM

Robert Creeley

It is all a rhythm
from the shutting
door, to the window
opening,

the seasons, the sun's
light, the moon,
the oceans, the
growing of things,

the mind in men
personal, recurring
in them again,
thinking the end

is not the end, the
time returning,
themselves dead but
someone else coming.

If in death I am dead,
then in life also
dying, dying . . .
And the women cry and die.

The little children
grow only to old men.
The grass dries,
the force goes.

But is met by another
returning, oh not mine,
not mine, and
in turn dies.

The rhythm which projects
from itself continuity
bending all to its force
from windsor to door
from ceiling to floor,
light at the opening,
dark at the closing.

BECAUSE GROWING A MUSTACHE WAS PRETTY TIRING

Kenneth Patchen

The little green blackbird's father always said:
"A bear and a bean and a bee in bed,
Only on Bogoslof Island can one still get
That good old-fashioned white brown bread!" This made a
Very deep impression on the little green blackbird,
So he decided to forget the whole thing.
But first he painted a stolen motorcycle on the sidewalk
And sold it to a nearsighted policeman.
By then of course the little green blackbird
Remembered that his father also did impressions
Of J. Greenstripe Whittier on freshly-painted parkbenches.
So he invited nineteen hundred rabbits over for dinner;
And they each brought him a tin-plated goldfish,
A handful of gloves, the drawing of a frosty breath,
And one of those decks of newfangled playing cards,
The kind that bite people. Well, when it came time
To go home, all nineteen thousand rabbits filed out
In a pregnant silence, that was broken only
By the sound of their low-pitched voices
Raised in speech. Whereupon the father
Of the little green blackbird quietly said:
"It is our sentence, to endure;
And our only crime, that we are here to serve it."

LIVING IS —

Piet Hein

Living is
  a thing you do
now or never —
  which do you?

IN MY OWN VILLAGE

Chasei
Translated by Peter Beilenson

In my own village
I think there are more scarecrows left
Than other people

There exists an obvious fact that seems utterly moral: namely, that a man is always a prey to his truths. Once he has admitted them, he cannot free himself from them. One has to pay something. A man who has become conscious of the absurd is forever bound to it. A man devoid of hope and conscious of being so has ceased to belong to the future. That is natural. But it is just as natural that he should strive to escape the universe of which he is the creator.

Albert Camus : *The Myth of Sisyphus*

A POISON TREE

William Blake

I was angry with my friend:
I told my wrath, my wrath did end.
I was angry with my foe:
I told it not, my wrath did grow.

And I water'd it in fears,
Night & morning with my tears;
And I sunned it with smiles,
And with soft deceitful wiles.

And it grew both day and night,
Till it bore an apple bright;
And my foe beheld it shine,
And he knew that it was mine,

And into my garden stole
When the night had veil'd the pole:
In the morning glad I see
My foe outstretch'd beneath the tree.

OUTWITTED

Edwin Markham

He drew a circle that shut me out —
Heretic, rebel, a thing to flout.
But Love and I had the wit to win:
We drew a circle that took him in!

ONE WHO HOPES

Kenneth Patchen

Born like a veritable living prince
With small, pink, rectangular feet
And a disposition to hair, I stand
Under the blazing moon and wonder
At the disappearance of all holy things
From this once so promising world;
And it does not much displease me
To be told that at seven tomorrow morning
An Angel of Justice will appear,
And that he will clean up people's messes for them —
Because if he is, and he does, he'll be more apt
To rub their lousy snouts in it.

DEATH OF A SON (WHO DIED IN A MENTAL HOSPITAL AGE ONE)

Jon Silkin

Something has ceased to come along with me.
Something like a person: something very like one.
    And there was no nobility in it
      Or anything like that.

    Something was there like a one year
Old house, dumb as stone. While the near buildings
      Sang like birds and laughed
      Understanding the pact

    They were to have with silence. But he
Neither sang nor laughed. He did not bless silence
      Like bread, with words.
      He did not forsake silence.

    But rather, like a house in mourning
Kept the eye turned in to watch the silence while
      The other houses like birds
      Sang around him.

And the breathing silence neither
Moved nor was still.

    I have seen stones: I have seen brick
But this house was made up of neither bricks nor stone
      But a house of flesh and blood
      With flesh of stone

    And bricks for blood. A house
Of stones and blood in breathing silence with the other
      Birds singing crazy on its chimneys.
      But this was silence,

    This was something else, this was
Hearing and speaking though he was a house drawn
      Into silence, this was
      Something religious in his silence,

    Something shining in his quiet,
This was different, this was altogether something else:
      Though he never spoke, this
      Was something to do with death.

    And then slowly the eye stopped looking
Inward. The silence rose and became still.
The look turned to the outer place and stopped,
      With the birds still shrilling around him.
      And as if he could speak

He turned over on his side with his one year
Red as a wound
He turned over as if he could be sorry for this
And out of his eyes two great tears rolled, like stones, and
    he died.

THE EMPEROR OF ICE-CREAM

Wallace Stevens

Call the roller of big cigars,
The muscular one, and bid him whip
In kitchen cups concupiscent curds.
Let the wenches dawdle in such dress
As they are used to wear, and let the boys
Bring flowers in last month's newspapers.
Let be be finale of seem.
The only emperor is the emperor of ice-cream.

Take from the dresser of deal,
Lacking the three glass knobs, that sheet
On which she embroidered fantails once
And spread it so as to cover her face.
If her horny feet protrude, they come
To show how cold she is, and dumb
Let the lamp affix its beam.
The only emperor is the emperor of ice-cream.

"BUFFALO BILL'S DEFUNCT"

e. e. cummings

Buffalo Bill's
defunct
            who used to
            ride a watersmooth-silver
                                        stallion
and break onetwothreefourfive pigeonsjustlikethat
                                                Jesus
he was a handsome man
                        and what i want to know is
how do you like your blueeyed boy
Mister Death

Hobbits are an unobtrusive but very ancient people, more numerous formerly than they are today; for they love peace and quiet and good tilled earth: a well-ordered and well-farmed countryside was their favourite haunt. They do not and did not understand or like machines more complicated than a forge-bellows, a water-mill, or a handloom, though they were skilful with tools. Even in ancient days they were, as a rule, shy of "the Big Folk," as they call us, and now they avoid us with dismay and are becoming hard to find. They are quick of hearing and sharp-eyed, and though they are inclined to be fat and do not hurry unnecessarily, they are nonetheless nimble and deft in their movements. They possessed from the first the art of disappearing swiftly and silently, when large folk whom they do not wish to meet come blundering by; and this art they have developed until to Men it may seem magical. But the Hobbits have never, in fact, studied magic of any kind, and their elusiveness is due solely to a professional skill that heredity and practice, and a close friendship with the earth, have rendered inimitable by bigger and clumsier races.

J. R. R. Tolkien : *The Fellowship of the Ring*

"In behaviouristic tradition, one picture image, seen by itself, impresses one fact on the mind. But two or three picture images seen simultaneously, and often with continuously changing juxtaposition, conjure up a complexity of ideas and relations in which the whole is clearly more than a sum of the parts. Much more of learning is subliminal than we ever guessed, and such multiple images seem to stimulate ideas in the mind. Later, these ideas can be recognized and retained in varying ways, dependent upon the recipient. The real question of how to evaluate the residue of such experiences has not been answered. IT HAS BEEN SUGGESTED THAT IT IS PRIMARILY A SENSORY AND EMOTIONAL EXPERIENCE, and not intellectual, which brings about changes in attitude rather than changes in philosophies."

Living and Learning

PRAYER

bp Nichol

teach me song. i
would sing. teach me
love. i would
i were open
to it. teach me
to pray
privately, praise
quietly
those things
i should. show me
the grace
of movement
& touch – that much
i would offer
to her. teach me
more – a way
for me
to reach her
who beckons
hesitantly. teach me
to be sure.

TO A YOUNG CHILD

Gerard Manley Hopkins

Margaret, are you grieving
Over Goldengrove unleaving?
Leaves, like the things of man, you
With your fresh thoughts care for, can you?
Ah! as the heart grows older
It will come to such sights colder
By and by, nor spare a sigh
Though worlds of wanwood leafmeal lie;
And yet you will weep and know why.
Now no matter, child, the name:
Sorrow's springs are the same.
Nor mouth had, no nor mind, expressed
What heart heard of, ghost guessed:
It is the blight man was born for.
It is Margaret you mourn for.

TABULA RASA

Issa

A little child
Picked with his fingers
A drop of dew –
And lo, it vanished!

NOTES FOR MY SON
(From *Song of Lazarus*)

Alex Comfort

Remember when you hear them beginning to say Freedom
Look carefully – see who it is that they want you to butcher.

Remember, when you say that the old trick would not have fooled you for a moment
That every time it is the trick which seems new.

Remember that you will have to put in irons
Your better nature, if it will desert to them.

Remember, remember their faces – watch them carefully:
For every step you take is on somebody's body

And every cherry you plant for them is a gibbet
And every furrow you turn for them is a grave

Remember, the smell of burning will not sicken you
If they persuade you that it will thaw the world

Beware. The blood of a child does not smell so bitter
If you have shed it with a high moral purpose.

So that because the woodcutter disobeyed
they will not burn her today or any day

So that for lack of a joiner's obedience
The crucifixion will not now take place

So that when they come to sell you their bloody corruption
You will gather the spit of your chest
And plant it in their faces.

THE WASHING OF THE INFANT

Su Shih

Most men, bringing up sons, wish for them intellect;
But I by my intellect have had a life-time of failure.
I would only desire that my child should be simple and dull,
That with no ill-fortune and no troubles he may attain to highest office.

"MY PARENTS KEPT ME..."

Stephen Spender

My parents kept me from children who were rough
Who threw words like stones and who wore torn clothes.
Their thighs showed through rags. They ran in the street
And climbed cliffs and stripped by the country streams.

I feared more than tigers their muscles like iron
Their jerking hands and their knees tight on my arms.
I feared the salt coarse pointing of those boys
Who copied my lisp behind me on the road.

They were lithe, they sprang out behind hedges
Like dogs to bark at my world. They threw mud
While I looked the other way, pretending to smile.
I longed to forgive them, but they never smiled.

The first lesson we ought to learn, the most important thing for us to know, is how to suffer. It seems as if children were formed small and feeble only to learn this important lesson without danger. . . .

Jean-Jacques Rousseau : *Emile*

NOTES

TO A SIXTH FORM READER

Paul Coltman
From the German of Hans Magnus Enzensberger

Do not read odes, my son. Be more exact.
Read timetables. Unroll sea charts and maps
before it is too late. Don't sing.
Be vigilant. The day is coming
when they again will nail up lists
on doors and brand upon the chest
those who say, No. Learn how to pass
unrecognized; and doing this
learn more than I did: how to change place,
cards of identity, your face.
Be skilled in little acts of treachery;
the furtive art of moving on each day.
Encyclicals are fine as fire lighters
and for defenceless people's salt and butter
a manifesto makes a handy wrapper.
But rage and patience, they are needed now
to blow into the open lungs of power
the powder ground, a fine and deadly dust,
by those like you who know and are meticulous.

BIRD IN THE CLASSROOM

Colin Thiele

The students drowsed and drowned
in the teacher's ponderous monotone –
Limp bodies looping in the wordy heat,
Melted and run together, desks and flesh as one,
Swooning and swimming in a sea of drone.

Each one asleep, swayed and vaguely drifted
With lidding eyes and lolling, weighted heads,
Was caught on heavy waves and dimly lifted,
Sunk slowly, ears ringing, in the syrup of his sound,
Or borne from the room on a heaving wilderness of beds.

And then, on a sudden, a bird's cool voice
Punched out song. Crisp and spare
On the startled air,
Beak-beamed
Or idly tossed,
Each note gleamed
Like a bead of frost.

A bird's cool voice from a neighbour tree
With five clear calls – mere grains of sound
Rare and neat
Repeated twice . . .
But they sprang the heat
Like drops of ice.

Ears cocked, before the comment ran
Fading and chuckling where a wattle stirred,
The students wondered how they could have heard
Such dreary monotones from man,
Such wisdom from a bird.

REMINDERS

We see that infants learn to speak in their own way in an environment where there is speaking and where they are addressed and take part. If we tried to teach children to speak according to our own theories and methods and schedules, as we try to teach reading, there would be as many stammerers as there are bad readers. Besides, it has been shown that whatever is useful in the present eight-year elementary curriculum can be learned in four months by a normal child of twelve. If let alone, in fact, he will have learned most of it by himself.

Paul Goodman : *Freedom and Learning*

What are the conditions of the creative attitude, of seeing and responding, of being aware and being sensitive to what one is aware of? First of all, it requires the capacity to be puzzled. Children still have the capacity to be puzzled. . . . But once they are through the process of education, most people lose the capacity of wondering, of being surprised. They feel they ought to know everything, and hence that it is a sign of ignorance to be surprised or puzzled by anything.

Erich Fromm : *The Art of Loving*

ABOUT SCHOOL

He always
He always wanted to explain things, but no one cared,
So he drew.

Sometimes he would just draw and it wasn't anything.
He wanted to carve it in stone or write it in the sky.
He would lie out on the grass and look up in the sky and it would
 be only the sky and things inside him that needed saying.

And it was after that that he drew the picture,
It was a beautiful picture. He kept it under his pillow and would
 let no one see it.
And he would look at it every night and think about it.
And when it was dark and his eyes were closed he could see it
 still.
And it was all of him and he loved it.

When he started school he brought it with him,
Not to show anyone, but just to have with him like a friend.

It was funny about school.
He sat in a square brown room, like all the other rooms,
And it was tight and close, and stiff.

He hated to hold the pencil and chalk, with his arm stiff and
 his feet flat on the floor, stiff, with the teacher watching
 and watching.

The teacher came and spoke to him.
She told him to wear a tie like all the other boys,
He said he didn't like them and she said it didn't matter.
After that he drew. And he drew all yellow and it was the way
 he felt about morning. And it was beautiful.

The teacher came and smiled at him. "What's this?" she said.
"Why don't you draw something like Ken's drawing?
 Isn't it beautiful?"

After that his mother bought him a tie and he always drew air-
 planes and rocket-ships like everyone else.
And he threw the old picture away.
And when he lay all alone looking at the sky, it was big and blue,
 and all of everything, but he wasn't anymore.

He was square and brown inside and his hands were stiff.
And he was like everyone else. All the things inside him that
 needed saying didn't need it anymore.

It had stopped pushing. It was crushed.
Stiff.
Like everything else .

WARNING TO CHILDREN

Robert Graves

Children, if you dare to think
Of the greatness, rareness, muchness,
Fewness of this precious only
Endless world in which you say
You live, you think of things like this:
Blocks of slate enclosing dappled
Red and green, enclosing tawny
Yellow nets, enclosing white
And black acres of dominoes,
Where a neat brown paper parcel
Tempts you to untie the string.
In the parcel a small island,
On the island a large tree,
On the tree a husky fruit.
Strip the husk and pare the rind off:
In the kernel you will see
Blocks of slate enclosed by dappled
Red and green, enclosed by tawny
Yellow nets, enclosed by white
And black acres of dominoes,
Where the same brown paper parcel
Children, leave the string alone!
For who dares to undo the parcel
Finds himself at once inside it,
On the island, in the fruit,
Blocks of slate about his head,
Finds himself enclosed by dappled
Green and red, enclosed by yellow
Tawny nets, enclosed by black
And white acres of dominoes,
With the same brown paper parcel
Still untied upon his knee.
And, if he then should dare to think
Of the fewness, muchness, rareness,
Greatness of this endless only
Precious world in which he says
He lives – he then unties the string.

LITTLE JOHNNY'S CONFESSION

Brian Patten

This morning
    being rather young and foolish
    I borrowed a machinegun my father
    had left hidden since the war, went out,
    and eliminated a number of small enemies.
    Since then I have not returned home.

This morning
    swarms of police with trackerdogs
    wander about the city
    with my description printed
    on their minds, asking:
    "Have you seen him,
    He is seven years old,
    likes Pluto, Mighty Mouse
    and Biffo the Bear,
    have you seen him anywhere?"

This morning
    sitting alone in a strange playground,
    muttering Youve blundered Youve blundered
    over and over to myself
    I work out my next move
    but cannot move;
    the trackerdogs will sniff me out,
    they have my lollypops.

DETAIL

William Carlos Williams

Hey!
Can I have some more
milk?
YEEEEAAAAASSSSS!
– always the gentle
mother!

QUESTIONS

THE LEAP

James Dickey

The only thing I have of Jane MacNaughton
Is one instant of a dancing-class dance.
She was the fastest runner in the seventh grade,
My scrapbook says, even when boys were beginning
To be as big as the girls,
But I do not have her running in my mind,
Though Frances Lane is there, Agnes Fraser,
Fat Betty Lou Black in the boys-against-girls
Relays we ran at recess: she must have run

Like the other girls, with her skirts tucked up
So they would be like bloomers,
But I cannot tell: that part of her is gone.
What I do have is when she came,
With the hem of her skirt where it should be
For a young lady, into the annual dance
Of the dancing class we all hated, and with a light
Grave leap, jumped up and touched the end
Of one of the paper-ring decorations

To see if she could reach it. She could,
And reached me now as well, hanging in my mind
From a brown chain of brittle paper, thin
And muscular, wide-mouthed, eager to prove
Whatever it proves when you leap
In a new dress, a new womanhood, among the boys
Whom you easily left in the dust
Of the passionless playground. If I said I saw
In the paper where Jane MacNaughton Hill,

Mother of four, leapt to her death from a window
Of a downtown hotel, and that her body crushed-in
The top of a parked taxi, and that I held
Without trembling a picture of her lying cradled
In that papery steel as though lying in the grass,
One shoe idly off, arms folded across her breast,
I would not believe myself. I would say
The convenient thing, that it was a bad dream
Of maturity, to see that eternal process

Most obsessively wrong with the world
Come out of her light, earth-spurning feet
Grown heavy: would say that in the dusty heels
Of the playground some boy who did not depend
On speed of foot, caught and betrayed her.
Jane, stay where you are in my first mind:
It was odd in that school, at that dance.
I and the other slow-footed yokels sat in corners
Cutting rings out of drawing paper

Before you leapt in your new dress
And touched the end of something I began,
Above the couples struggling on the floor,
New men and women clutching at each other
And prancing foolishly as bears: hold on
To that ring I made for you, Jane –
My feet are nailed to the ground
By dust I swallowed thirty years ago –
While I examine my hands.

HOMEWORK

SCHOOLCHILDREN

W. H. Auden

Here are all the captivities; the cells are as real:
But these are unlike the prisoners we know
Who are outraged or pining or wittily resigned
    Or just wish all away.

For they dissent so little, so nearly content
With the dumb play of the dog, the licking and rushing;
The bars of love are so strong, their conspiracies
    Weak like the vows of drunkards.

Indeed their strangeness is difficult to watch:
The condemned see only the fallacious angels of a vision;
So little effort lies behind their smiling,
    The beast of vocation is afraid.

But watch them, O, set against our size and timing
The almost neuter, the slightly awkward perfection;
For the sex is there, the broken bootlace is broken,
    The professor's dream is not true.

Yet the tyranny is so easy. The improper word
Scribbled upon the fountain, is that all the rebellion?
The storm of tears shed in the corner, are these
    The seeds of the new life?

THE DIVINE IMAGE

William Blake

To Mercy, Pity, Peace, and Love
All pray in their distress;
And to these virtues of delight
Return their thankfulness.

For Mercy, Pity, Peace, and Love
Is God, our father dear,
And Mercy, Pity, Peace, and Love
Is man, his child and care.

For Mercy has a human heart,
Pity a human face,
And Love, the human form divine,
And Peace, the human dress.

Then every man, of every clime
That prays in his distress,
Prays in the human form divine,
Love, Mercy, Pity, Peace.

And all must love the human form,
In heathen, Turk or Jew;
Where Mercy, Love, & Pity dwell
There God is dwelling too.

It may be that some of The Children of Change see themselves as Avenging Angels or fleshly manifestations of Prince Valiant, whose job on Earth is to exorcise the "demons" of hypocrisy. Or, perhaps, it is The Children of Change who are themselves the demons. Who, this early, can tell?

    Don Fabun : *Dynamics of Change*

Although we experience the world in bits and pieces, the sequence in which we experience them flows together and we feel the world around us as a continuous panorama. When we try to communicate about it, we have to break it down into bits and pieces. Perhaps a large part of our trouble starts there.

    Don Fabun : *Communications*

Three statements are usually made about the effects of early experience. The first is that early habits are very persistent and may prevent the formation of new ones. This, of course, refers not only to the study of experimental animals but also the rearing of children. The second statement is that early perceptions deeply affect all future learning. This concept leads to the difficult question whether basic perceptions – the way we have of seeing the world around us – are inherited or acquired. The third statement is simply that early social contacts determine adult social behavior. This, of course, is imprinting.

    Eckhard H. Hess : *"Imprinting in Animals"*

MY PAPA'S WALTZ

Theodore Roethke

The whiskey on your breath
Could make a small boy dizzy;
But I hung on like death:
Such waltzing was not easy.

We romped until the pans
Slid from the kitchen shelf;
My mother's countenance
Could not unfrown itself.

The hand that held my wrist
Was battered on one knuckle;
At every step you missed
My right ear scraped a buckle.

You beat time on my head
With a palm caked hard by dirt,
Then waltzed me off to bed
Still clinging to your shirt.

How can happiness be bestowed? My own answer is: Abolish authority. Let the child be himself. Don't push him around. Don't teach him. Don't lecture him. Don't elevate him. Don't force him to do anything. It may not be your answer. But if you reject my answer, it is incumbent on you to find a better one.

A. S. Neill : *Summerhill*

A parent is a specialist who never had any training as a specialist.

A. S. Neill : *Freedom – Not License!*

DEFINITIONS

THE RIGHTEOUS MOTHER

Eden Phillpotts

"Wretch!" cried the mother to her infant son.
"You hateful little boy, what have you done?
Killed the white butterfly, of all dear things,
And then pulled off his tiny, fairy wings.
To butterflies this garden is their home –
Here do they dance and kiss the flowers and roam
In happiness and plenty, even as you.
God would be very angry if He knew!"
And while she spoke these salutary words
Her hat displayed two withered humming-birds.

THE LESSON

Edward Lucie-Smith

"Your father's gone," my bald headmaster said.
His shiny dome and brown tobacco jar
Splintered at once in tears. It wasn't grief.
I cried for knowledge which was bitterer
Than any grief. For there and then I knew
That grief has uses – that a father dead
Could bind the bully's fist a week or two;
And then I cried for shame, then for relief.

I was a month past ten when I learnt this:
I still remember how the noise was stilled
In school-assembly when my grief came in.
Some goldfish in a bowl quietly sculled
Around their shining prison on its shelf.
They were indifferent. All the other eyes
Were turned towards me. Somewhere in myself
Pride, like a goldfish, flashed a sudden fin.

THE SECRET HEART
Robert P. Tristram Coffin

Across the years he could recall
His father one way best of all.

In the stillest hour of night
The boy awakened to a light

Half in dreams, he saw his sire
With his great hands full of fire

The man had struck a match to see
If his son slept peacefully.

He held his palms each side the spark
His love had kindled in the dark.

His two hands were curved apart
In the semblance of a heart.

He wore, it seemed to his small son,
A bare heart on his hidden one,

A heart that gave out such a glow
No son awake could bear to know.

It showed a look upon a face
Too tender for the day to trace.

One instant, it lit all about,
And then the secret heart went out.

But it shone long enough for one
To know that hands held up the sun.

THE MAN WHO FINDS THAT HIS SON HAS BECOME A THIEF
Raymond Souster

Coming into the store at first angry
At the accusation, believing in
The word of his boy who has told him:
I didn't steal anything, honest.

Then becoming calmer, seeing that anger
Will not help in the business, listening painfully
As the other's evidence unfolds, so painfully slow.

Then seeing gradually that evidence
Almost as if tightened slowly around the neck
Of his son, at first vaguely circumstantial, then
    gathering damage,
Until there is present the unmistakable odour of guilt
Which now seeps into the mind and lays its poison.

Suddenly feeling sick and alone and afraid,
As if an unseen hand had slapped him in the face
For no reason whatsoever: wanting to get out
Into the street, the night, the darkness, anywhere to hide
The pain that must show in the face to these strangers,
    the fear.

It must be like this,
It could hardly be otherwise.

Western philosophers have always gone on the assumption that fact is something cut and dried, precise, immobile, very convenient, and ready for examination. The Chinese deny this. The Chinese believe that a fact is something crawling and alive, a little furry and cool to the touch, that crawls down the back of your neck.

    Lin Yutang

CORNER

Ralph Pomeroy

The cop slumps alertly on his motorcycle,
Supported by one leg like a leather stork,
His glance accuses me of loitering.
I can see his eyes moving like fish
In the green depths of his green goggles.

His ease is fake. I can tell.
My ease is fake. And he can tell.
The fingers armoured by his gloves,
Splay and clench, itching to change something.
As if he were my enemy or my death,
I just stand there watching.

I spit out my gum which has gone stale.
I knock out a new cigarette –
Which is my bravery/
It is all imperceptible
The way I shift my weight,
The way he creaks in his saddle.

The traffic is specific though constant.
The sun surrounds me, divides the street between us
His crash helmet is white in the shade.
It is like a bull ring as they say it is just before the fighting
I cannot back down. I am there.

Everything holds me back/
I am in danger of disappearing into the sunny dust.
My levis bake and my T shirt sweats.

My cigarette makes my eyes burn
But I don't dare drop it.
Who made him my enemy?
Prince of coolness. King of Fear
Why do I lean here waiting?
Why does he lounge there watching?

I am becoming sunlight
My hair is on fire, my boots run like tar.
I am hung-up by the bright air.

Something breaks through all of a sudden,
And he blasts off, quick as a craver,
Smug is his power; watching me watch.

JUSTICE 111: SOCIAL NOTES

F. R. Scott

This judge is busy sentencing criminals
Of whose upbringing and environment he is totally ignorant.
His qualifications, however, are the highest –
A B.A. degree,
A technical training in Law,
Ten years practice at the Bar,
And membership in the right political party.
Who should know better than he
Just how many years in prison
Will reform a slum-product,
Or whether ten or twenty strokes of the lash
Will put an end to assaults on young girls?

EDUCATION A FAILURE

William Carlos Williams

The minor stupidities
of my world
dominate that world –
as when

with two bridges across
the river and one
closed for repairs
the other also

will be closed by
the authorities
for painting! But then
there is heaven

and the ideal state
closed also
before the aspiring soul.
I had rather

watch a cat threading
a hedge with
another sitting by
while the bird

screams overhead
athrash
in the cover of the
low branches.

THE EXECUTION

Alden Knowlan

On the night of the execution
a man at the door
mistook me for the coroner.
"Press," I said.

But he didn't understand. He led me
into the wrong room
where the sheriff greeted me:
"You're late, Padre."

"You're wrong," I told him. "I'm Press."
"Yes, of course, Reverend Press."
We went down the stairway.

"Ah, Mr. Ellis," said the Deputy.
"Press!" I shouted. But he shoved me
through a black curtain.
The lights were so bright
I couldn't see the faces
of the men sitting
opposite. But, thank God, I thought
they can see me!

"Look!" I cried. "Look at my face!
Doesn't anybody know me?"

Then a hood covered my head.
"Don't make it harder for us," the hangman whispered.

THUG

Raymond Garlick

School began it.
There he felt
the tongue's salt lash
raising its welt

on a child's heart.
Ten years ruled
by violence left him
thoroughly schooled,

nor did he fail
to understand
the blow of the
headmaster's hand.

That hand his hand
round the cosh curled.
What rules the classroom
rocks the world.

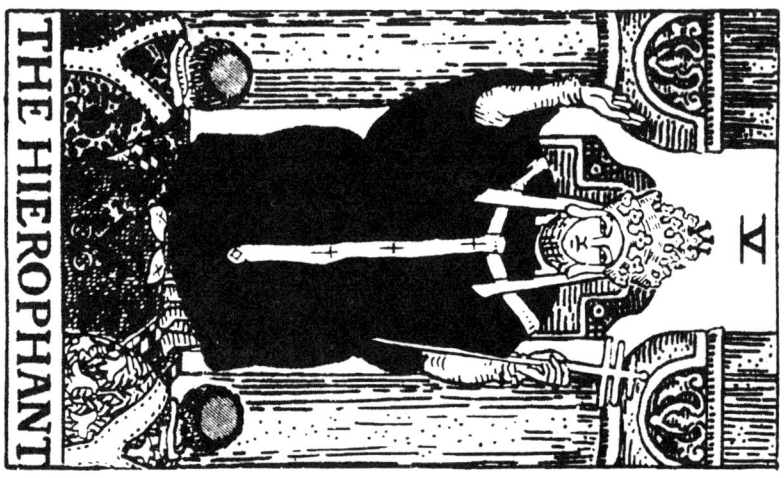

[Aldous Huxley] compared the brain to a "reducing valve." In ordinary perception, the senses send an overwhelming flood of information to the brain, which the brain then filters down to a trickle it can manage for the purpose of survival in a highly competitive world. Man has become so rational, so utilitarian, that the trickle becomes most pale and thin. It is efficient, for mere survival, but it screens out the most wondrous part of man's potential experience without his even knowing it. *We're shut off from our own world.* Primitive man once experienced the rich and sparkling flood of the senses fully. Children experience it for a few months – until "normal" training, conditioning, close the doors on this other world, usually for good.

Tom Wolfe : *The Electric Kool-Aid Acid Test*

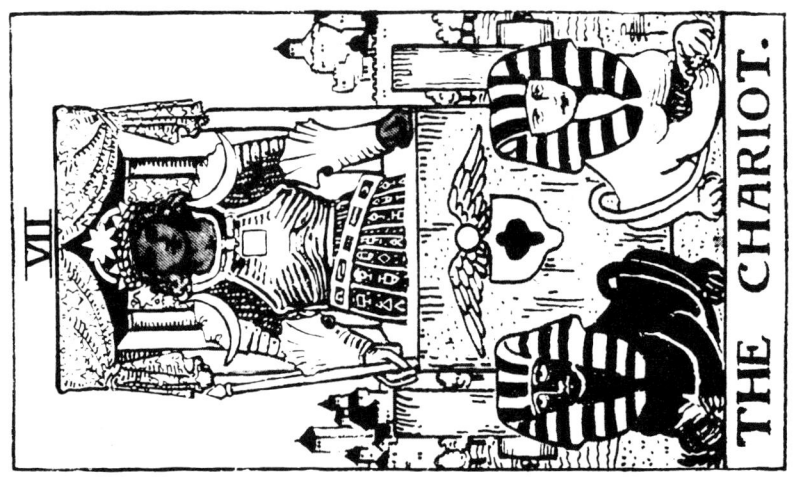

It is a difficult thing to know when to give and when to take, when to turn the other cheek and when to let the other guy have it. Law-givers and law-enforcers often give advice on the matter, but then so do yippies and rock stars, and fathers and mothers, along with many others. However, it is interesting to find how seldom poets – or other artists – tell you what to do. They put you in an experience where you see and feel, but you still have to decide for yourself what to do.

On the other hand, institutions usually can tell you when or how to give and take. The state especially, that institution which claims to contain all other institutions, tells you what to do – or, more often, what not to do. But since all institutions, especially the state, have as one of their principal though often unstated aims the perpetuation of their own power and structure, their laws are often suspect. You can find more truth in a poem than in a government regulation. But then, most of what other people or institutions advise you is not going to jar you; it is only the advice of a few that can hurt. So most of us, deciding alone, usually find ourselves in the position of American Senator Thomas Dodd, who plaintively said . . .

THERE OUGHT TO BE A LAW SO A MAN KNOWS WHETHER HE'S DOING RIGHT OR WRONG.

Here are no laws but some poems.
You must still decide for yourself.

COMPLAINT LODGED WITH L.C.B.O. BY A CITIZEN IN UPPER RUMBELOW
Alfred Purdy

I am driving thru town with a case
of beer in the back seat
with two empties in it
which is illegal see and
I notice this cop in the rear
vision mirror following me on
a motor cycle and for a minute
I feel peculiar –
At the stop street I carefully
STOP
       and the cop stops not
to be caught that easy
and I see him watching me
sit so I sit up straight as
"The Motorist" by Praxiteles
excavated by Henry Ford 4
from under a million traffic tickets
of dead Greeks speeding in Argos agora
or was it "Hermes" or "Pallas Athene"
and not "The Motorist" at all
                      Anyway
there's that cop on my tail
and I signal a left turn
and he signals a left turn
I signal a right turn
and he signals a right turn
and I think what the hell
is this a game or something and
maybe didn't I brush my teeth
this morning and grin at him anyway
in the rear view mirror and figure
out a hand signal for a ground
loop and inverted immelmann plus an
unorthodox Christiana I learned
once on Parnassus which lofts
me among the treetops there encountering
God (hi pops) 50 feet above the
business section we stop and talk and
I ask him about that damned cop
of his and (ha ha) how I fooled him –

But he's parked waiting for me
at the Presbyterian steeple
that got struck by lightning like
a blue cop-angel who's a
dead ringer for the prophet Isaiah
and I says "You didn't make the turn signal"
and he says "It ain't in the book"
and I guess that's so it ain't so
I get fined fifteen bucks
and let off with a warning
but just the same –

PROTOCOLS

(BIRKENAU, ODESSA: THE CHILDREN SPEAK ALTERNATELY)

Randall Jarrell

We went there on the train. *They had big barges that they towed,*
We stood up, there were so many I was squashed.
There was a smoke-stack, then they made me wash.
It was a factory, I think. *My mother held me up*
And I could see the ship that made the smoke.

When I was tired my mother carried me.
She said, "Don't be afraid." But I was only tired.
Where we went there is no more Odessa.
They had water in a pipe – like rain, but hot;
The water there is deeper than the world

And I was tired and fell in in my sleep
And the water drank me. That is what I think.
And I said to my mother, "Now I'm washed and dried,"
My mother hugged me, and it smelled like hay
And that is how you die. And that is how you die.

FAMILY HISTORY

Jacques Prévert
translated by E. A. Lacey

The mother knits
and the son goes to war
and the mother thinks "That's what sons are for."
And the father? What does the father do?
He runs a store.
His wife does knitting
his son goes to war
he goes to the store –
and the father thinks "That's what men are for."
And the son? The son and heir?
What does he think, the son and heir?
Why, nothing at all. He doesn't care.
His mother does knitting,
his father keeps store,
he makes war.
When he is through making war
he and his father will run the store.
On knits the mother,
on goes the war,
on goes the father running the store.
But the son is killed: he goes on no more.
So the mother and father go in their car
to the churchyard and think "That's the way things are."
And life goes on, with knitting and wars
and stores
wars and stores and knitting and wars
and stores and stores and stores
and wars.

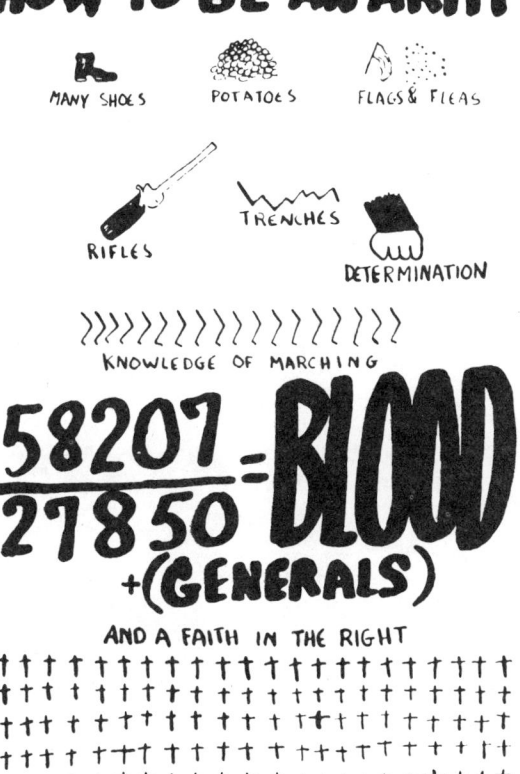

SIX YOUNG MEN

Ted Hughes

The celluloid of a photograph holds them well, –
Six young men, familiar to their friends.
Four decades that have faded and ochre-tinged
This photograph have not wrinkled the faces or the hands.
Though their cocked hats are not now fashionable,
Their shoes shine. One imparts an intimate smile,
One chews a grass, one lowers his eyes, bashful,
One is ridiculous with a cocky pride –
Six months after this picture they were all dead.

All are trimmed for a Sunday jaunt. I know
That bilberried bank, that thick tree, that black wall,
Which are there yet and not changed. From where these sit
You hear the water of seven streams fall
To the roarer in the bottom, and through all
The leafy valley a rumouring of air go.
Pictured here, their expressions listen yet,
And still that valley has not changed its sound
Though their faces are four decades under the ground.

This one was shot in an attack and lay
Calling in the wire, then this one, his best friend,
Went out to bring him in and was shot too;
And this one, the very moment he was warned
From potting at tin-cans in no-man's land,
Fell back dead with his rifle-sights shot away.
The rest, nobody knows what they came to,
But come to the worst they must have done, and held it
Closer than their hope; all were kind.

Here see a man's photograph,
The locket of a smile, turned overnight
Into the hospital of his mangled last
Agony and hours; see bundled in it
His mightier-than-a-man dead bulk and weight:
And on this one place which keeps him alive
(In his Sunday best) see fall war's worst
Thinkable flash and rending, onto his smile
Forty years rotting into soil.

That man's not more alive whom you confront
And shake by the hand, see hale, hear speak loud,
Then any of these six celluloid smiles are,
Nor prehistoric or fabulous beast more dead;
No thought so vivid as their smoking blood:
To regard this photograph might well dement,
Such contradictory permanent horrors here
Smile from the single exposure and shoulder out
One's own body from its instant and heat.

HAVE YOU KILLED YOUR MAN FOR TODAY?

Kenneth Patchen

In these hands, the cities; in my weather, the armies
Of better things than die
To the scaly music of war.

The different men, who are dead,
Had cunning; they sought green lives
In a world blacker than your world;
But you have nourished the taste of sickness
Until all other tastes are dull in your mouths;
It is only we who stand outside the steaming tents
Of hypocrisy and murder
Who are "sick" –

This is the health you want.

Yours is the health of the pig which roots up
The vines that would give him food;
Our is the sickness of the deer which is shot
Because it is the activity of hunters to shoot him.

In your hands, the cities; in my world, the marching
Of nobler feet than walk down a road
Deep with the corpses of every sane and beautiful thing.

THE MAN IN THE DEAD MACHINE

Donald Hall

High on a slope in New Guinea
the Grumman Hellcat
lodges among bright vines
as thick as arms. In 1942
the clenched hand of a pilot
glided it here
where no one has ever been.

In the cockpit the helmeted
skeleton sits
upright, held
by dry sinews at neck
and shoulder, and webbing
that straps the pelvic cross
to the cracked
leather of the seat, and the breastbone
of the parachute.

Or say that the shrapnel
missed him, he flew
back to the carrier, and every
morning takes his chair, his pale
hands on the black arms, and sits
upright, held
by the firm webbing.

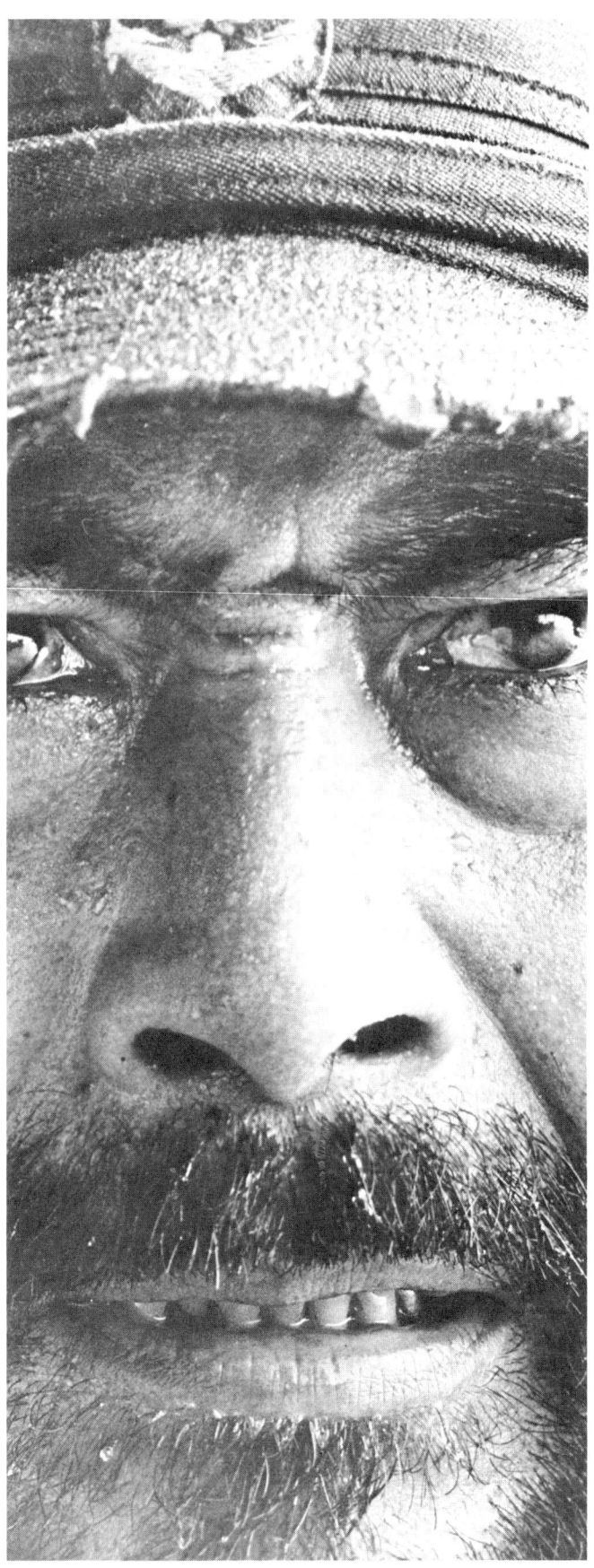

AFTERTHOUGHTS ON A NAPALM-DROP ON JUNGLE VILLAGES NEAR HAIPHONG

Barbara Beidler

All was still.
The sun rose through silver pine boughs,
Over sleeping green-straw huts,
Over cool rice ponds,
Through the emerald jungles,
Into the sky.

The men rose and went out to the fields and ponds.
The women set pots on the fire, boiling rice and jungle berries,
    and some with baskets went for fish.
The children played in the streams and danced through the weeds.

Then there was the flash – silver and gold
Silver and gold,
Silver birds flying
Golden water raining.
The rice ponds blazed with the new water.
The jungles burst into gold and sent up little birds of fire.
Little animals with fur of flame.

Then the children flamed.
Running – their clothes flying like firey kites.
Screaming – their screams dying as their faces seared.
The women's baskets burned on their heads.

The men's boats blazed on the rice waters.
Then the rains came.
A rag, fire black, fluttered.
A curl of smoke rose from a lone rice stem.
The forest lay singed, seared.
A hut crumbled.

And all was still.

   Listen, Americans,
   Listen, clear and long.
   The children are screaming
   In the jungles of Haiphong.

. . . whatever brotherhood human beings may be capable of has grown out of fratricide, whatever political organization men may have achieved has its origin in crime. The conviction, In the beginning was a crime – for which the phrase "state of nature" is only a theoretically purified para-phrase – has carried through the centuries no less self-evident plausibility for the state of human affairs than the first sentence of St. John, "In the beginning was the Word," has possessed for the affairs of salvation.

Hannah Arendt : *On Revolution*

"SAY THIS CITY HAS TEN MILLION SOULS"

W. H. Auden

Say this city has ten million souls,
Some are living in mansions, some are living in holes:
Yet there's no place for us, my dear, yet there's no place for us.

Once we had a country and we thought it fair,
Look in the atlas and you'll find it there:
We cannot go there now, my dear, we cannot go there now.

In the village churchyard there grows an old yew,
Every spring it blossoms anew:
Old passports can't do that, my dear, old passports can't do that.

The consul banged the table and said:
"If you've got no passport you're officially dead";
But we are still alive, my dear, but we are still alive.

Went to a committee; they offered me a chair;
Asked me politely to return next year:
But where shall we go to-day, my dear, but where shall we go to-day?

Came to a public meeting; the speaker got up and said:
"If we let them in, they will steal our daily bread";
He was talking of you and me, my dear, he was talking of you and me.

Thought I heard the thunder rumbling in the sky;
It was Hitler over Europe saying: "They must die";
O we were in his mind, my dear, O we were in his mind.

Saw a poodle in a jacket fastened with a pin,
Saw a door opened and a cat let in:
But they weren't German Jews, my dear, but they weren't German Jews.

Went down the harbour and stood upon the quay,
Saw the fish swimming as if they were free:
Only ten feet away, my dear, only ten feet away.

Walked through a wood, saw the birds in the trees;
They had no politicians and sang at their ease:
They weren't the human race, my dear, they weren't the human race.

Dreamed I saw a building with a thousand floors
A thousand windows and a thousand doors;
Not one of them was ours, my dear, not one of them was ours.

Stood on a great plain in the falling snow;
Ten thousand soldiers marched to and fro:
Looking for you and me, my dear, looking for you and me.

INNOCENCE
(TO TONY WHITE)
Thom Gunn

He ran the course and as he ran he grew,
And smelt his fragrance in the field. Already,
Running he knew the most he ever knew,
The egotism of a healthy body.

Ran into manhood, ignorant of the past:
Culture of guilt and guilt's vague heritage,
Self-pity and the soul; what he possessed
Was rich, potential, like the bud's tipped rage.

The Corps developed, it was plain to see,
Courage, endurance, loyalty, and skill
To a morale firm as morality,
Hardening him to an instrument, until

The finitude of virtues that were there
Bodied within the swarthy uniform
A compact innocence, child-like and clear,
No doubt could penetrate, no act could harm.

When he stood near the Russian partisan
Being burned alive, he therefore could behold
The ribs wear gently through the darkening skin
And sicken only at the Northern cold,

Could watch the fat burn with a violent flame
And feel disgusted only at the smell,
And judge that all pain finishes the same
As melting quietly by his boots it fell.

THE DEATH OF THE BALL TURRET GUNNER

Randall Jarrell

From my mother's sleep I fell into the State,
And I hunched in its belly till my wet fur froze.
Six miles from earth, loosed from its dream of life,
I woke to black flak and the nightmare fighters.
When I died they washed me out of the turret with a hose.

A SATYRICAL ELEGY ON THE DEATH
OF A LATE FAMOUS GENERAL, 1722

Jonathan Swift

His Grace! impossible! what, dead!
Of old age, too, and in his bed!
And could that mighty warrior fall,
And so inglorious, after all?
Well, since he's gone, no matter how,
The last loud trump must wake him now;
And, trust me, as the noise grows stronger,
He'd wish to sleep a little longer.
And could he be indeed so old
As by the newspapers we're told?
Threescore, I think, is pretty high;
'Twas time, in conscience he should die!
This world he cumber'd long enough;
He burnt his candle to the snuff;
And that's the reason, some folks think,
He left behind so great a stink.
Behold his funeral appears,
Nor widow's sighs, nor orphan's tears,
Wont at such times each heart to pierce,
Attend the progress of his hearse.
And what of that? his friends may say,
He had those honours in his day.
True to his profit and his pride,
He made them weep before he died.
   Come hither, all ye empty things,
Ye bubbles raised by breath of kings!
Who float upon the tide of state;
Come hither, and behold your fate.
Let Pride be taught by this rebuke,
How very mean a thing's a duke;
From all his ill-got honours flung,
Turn'd to that dirt from whence he sprung.

ON BEING ASKED FOR A WAR POEM

William Butler Yeats

I think it better that in times likes these
A poet's mouth be silent, for in truth
We have no gift to set a statesman right;
He has had enough of meddling who can please
A young girl in the indolence of her youth,
Or an old man upon a winter's night.

Around a man who has been pushed into the limelight, a legend begins to grow as it does around a dead one. But a dead man is in no danger of yielding to the temptation to nourish his legend, or accept its picture as reality. I pity the man who falls in love with his image as it is drawn by public opinion during the honeymoon of publicity.

    Dag Hammarskjold : *Markings*

WHY PATRIOTS ARE A BIT NUTS IN THE HEAD

Roger McGough

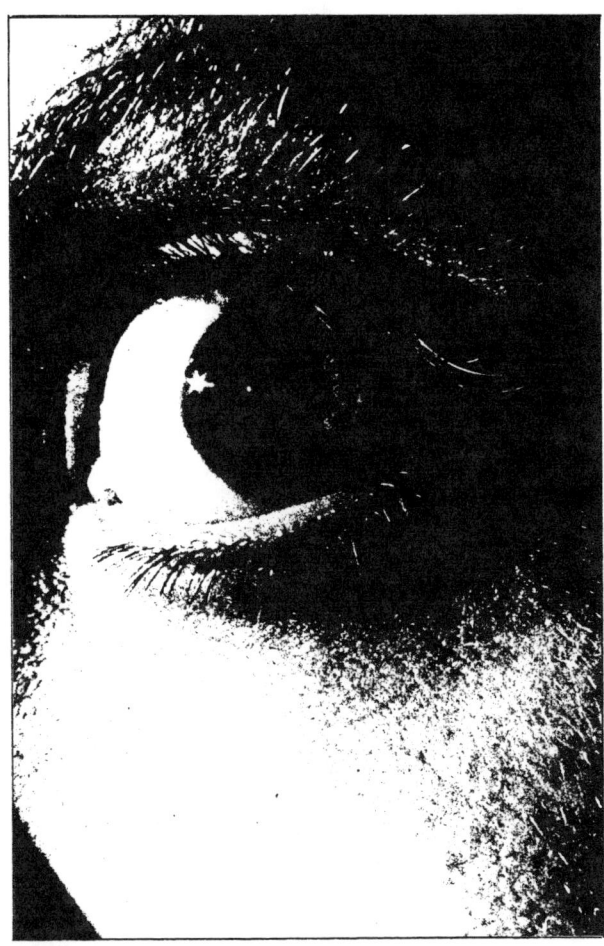

Patriots are a bit nuts in the head
because they wear
red, white and blue –
tinted spectacles
(red for blood
white for glory
and blue . . .
for a boy)
and are in effervescent danger
of losing their lives
lives are good for you
when you are alive
you can eat and drink a lot
and go out with girls
(sometimes if you are lucky
you can even go to bed with them)
but you can't do this
if you have your belly shot away
and your seeds
spread over some corner of a foreign field
to facilitate
in later years
the growing of oats by some peasant yobbo

when you are posthumous it is cold and dark
and that is why patriots are a bit nuts in the head

DEMOLITION

Norman Iles

I thank the amoeba for
My stomach juice's wonderful flow;
The fish for my backbone;
The frog for lungs;
And all animals together
For my strong skeleton;
Last, the tree-foot apes,
And all simians,
For my lobed brain
And instrumental thumbs.

And I report to them
That we, their heirs,
May, with our bomb,
Destroy the fruit of millions of years,
Our children;
Ourselves, as well, of course,
And, incidentally, all them.

I believe in compulsory cannibalism. If people were forced to eat what they killed, there would be no more wars.
    Abby Hoffman : *Revolutionforthehellofit*

Parnell picking up the front man and holding him an instant above his head flung him against the advancing crowd. MacDoon rotating his staff over his head and they said get that little bastard of a helicopter and Mac neatly broke the man's nose. The kangaroo reached behind the bar and was draining a bottle of gin when a chair was lowered on his head from behind. The kangaroo fell spread-eagled to the floor. Parnell attacked from all sides with MacDoon pulling them off with the hook of the staff and beating them to the floor. The building trembling. Eight left of the fourteen, six unconscious under the trampling feet. MacDoon went down and they were kicking him and he was catching them by the ankles with the hook and tripping them to the ground. They were driving Parnell out the door and they were yelling these damn Oxford intellectuals think they can tell us we're pigs. They had Parnell out and drew the latches. They were dragging the unconscious figure of MacDoon to fling him on the street, saying we fixed that big fella, he'll not try that again. Outside a great war whoop. They turned to the door. Another war whoop and a voice yelling I'm coming through. The brown vomit-tinted door parted with a squeal of hinges and splintering wood. The door came asunder into the room. Parnell, face covered in blood, clothes in tatters, launched his ferocious counter attack and three of the remaining eight fled up the stairs crying the man is insane, call the bobbies. They were holding him off with chairs. A crowd gathering on the street. The sound of the police. A half-revived MacDoon and Parnell dragging the stricken kangaroo out the door stumbling into the street. Flinging the beast into a taxi and yelling into the terrified man's ear, away you Cockney bastard like the hounds of hell before we deliver the wrath of the Celts on your English skull.

J. P. Donleavy : *The Ginger Man*

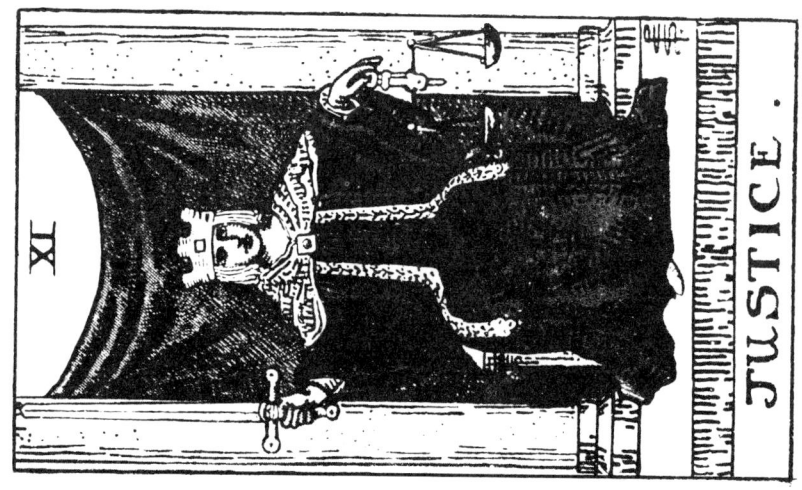

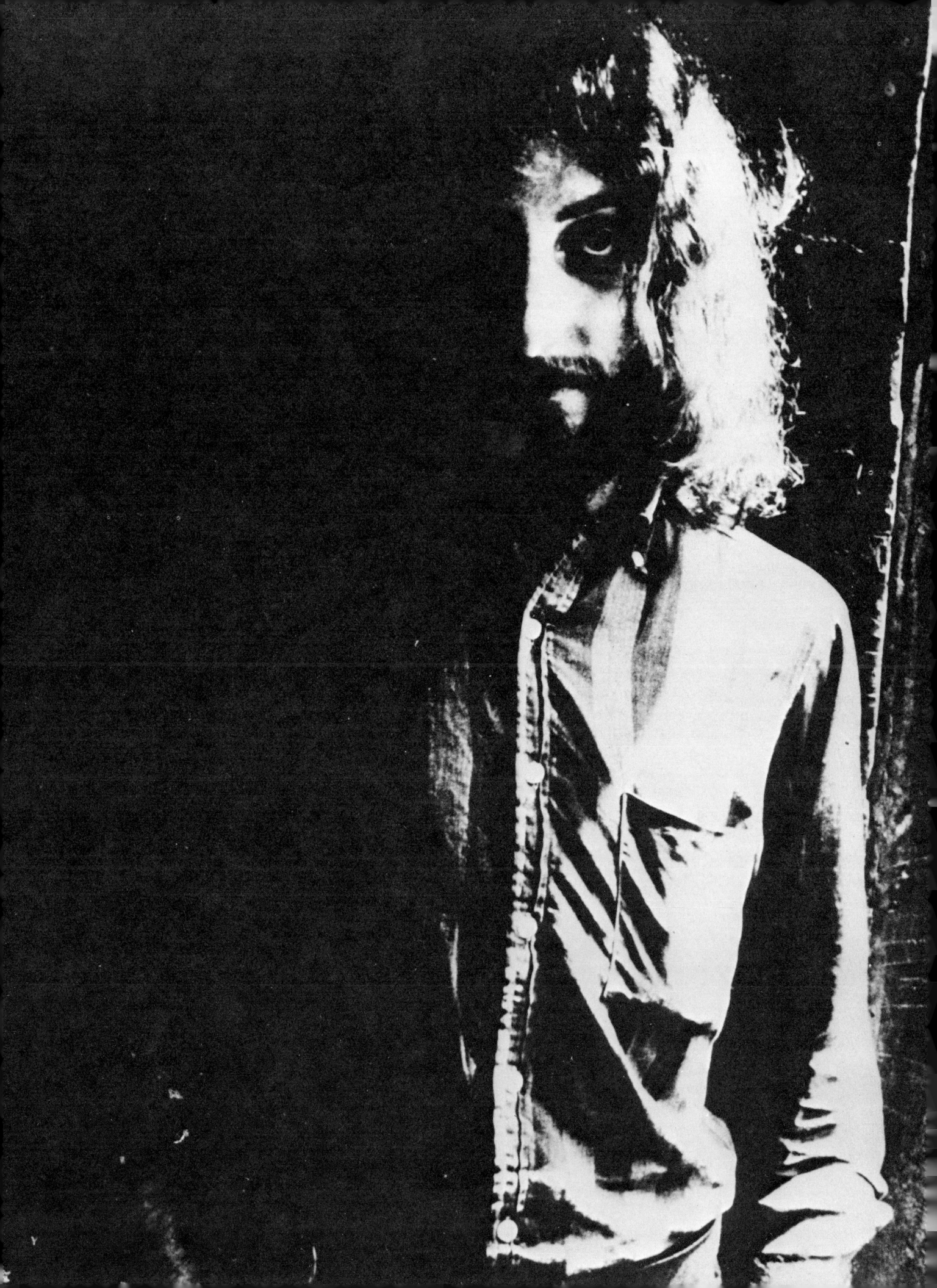

As we live, we cast away: breath and bodily substance,
clothing and articles,
things said and made,
unsaid and dreamed . . .

And we have just discovered it at large! Before, like sea creatures oblivious to the water they live in, we lived indifferent to the track of waste behind us. We built and destroyed, consumed and built again. Civilization and art. We left in our wake the detritus by which the next generation knew their ancestors and found a way of life. We lived through garbage, producing it, storing it, building upon it and around it. Now, we see it. We contemplate it, analyze it, classify it – and try to use it. We have museums and schools and factories to process it and to teach us to process it in turn. For the first time, we are trying, on a large scale, to use it. Some are even trying to avoid producing it. But that is an impossibility as long as we live and move and rest and die. But using it – that is all we have. So use it we must.

We find ourselves now in the garb-age. We are starting to pay attention to how the external relates to the internal, what covering means to what is covered. How something works is being connected, once again, to the style that it has and the use that it fulfills: clothing and nudity,   living and learning,
seeing and saying,   advertising and marketing,
packaging and shipping, you and me . . . and them.

It is no mistake, then, that today we worry about alienation. In this, the garb-age, as we pick our way through pits of garbage to learn the human use of garbage, we return to where we always begin, to the garbage-making animal. And we turn to those who were thought to be garbage, to the outsiders and the weirdos and the alienated. Now we suspect that some of them might have some special viewpoint that can help us see through our own detritus. From the dislocated we might find how to locate ourselves. From those who are OUT OF PLACE IN TIME AND SPACE – SAINTS
PSYCHOS
SYBILS
FREAKS

– we can learn to use our . . . . GARBAGE

LET US HAVE MADNESS

Kenneth Patchen

Let us have madness openly, O men
Of my generation. Let us follow
The footsteps of this slaughtered age:
See it trail across Time's dim land
Into the closed house of eternity
With the noise that dying has,
With the face that dead things wear – nor ever say

We wanted more; we looked to find
An open door, an utter deed of love,
Transforming day's evil darkness;
but
We found extended hell and fog
Upon the earth, and within the head
A rotting bog of lean huge graves.

WHERE ARE YOU NOW, BATMAN?

Brian Patten

Where are you now, Batman? Now that Aunt Heriot has
    reported Robin missing
And Superman's fallen asleep in the sixpenny childhood
    seats?
Where are you now that Captain Marvel's *SHAZAM!*
    echoes round the auditorium,
The magicians don't hear it,
Must all be deaf . . . or dead . . .
The Purple Monster who came down from the Purple
    planet disguised as a man
Is wandering aimlessly about the streets
With no way of getting back.

Sir Galahad's been strangled by the Incredible Living
        Trees,
Zorro killed by his own sword.
Blackhawk has buried the last of his companions
And has now gone off to commit suicide in the disused
        Hangars of Innocence.
The Monster and the Ape still fight it out in a room
Where the walls are continually closing in;
Rocketman's fuel tanks gave out over London.
Even Flash Gordon's lost, he wanders among the stars
Weeping over the woman he loved
7 Universes ago.
        My celluloid companions, it's only a few
                years
Since I knew you. Something in us has faded.
        Has the Terrible Fiend, That Ghastly
                Adversary,
Mr. Old Age, Caught you in his deadly trap,
And come finally to polish you off,
His machinegun dripping with years. . . ?

IN HIS FOOTSTEPS

Paul Hart

Your pregnant womb
balloons with genesis.
You wonder what pain
must be laboured through
before the first attempts to cry
burst forth.
Now,
as you watch his thriving legs
run-and-jump through hopscotched days,
you remember the hospital,
full of first and last cries,
hygiene and hygiene-white walls.
One day he breaks the window
you watched him through,
and you remember fearing
someone would teach him destruction
start him on the path of his father
in the nightmare yard where he raped you.

Psychosis is a state of absolute narcissism, one in which the person has broken all connection with reality outside, and has made his own person the substitute for reality. He is entirely filled with himself, he has become "god and the world" to himself. It is precisely this insight by which Freud for the first time opened the way to the dynamic understanding of the nature of psychosis.

Erich Fromm : *The Heart of Man*

NAPLES (AP) – He's known as Agostino the Madman. He does motorcycle acrobatics at midnight in teeming downtown Naples.

He did it again last night, to the delight of several thousand fans, and the outrage of out-classed police who couldn't catch his souped-up Ducati 125.

While numerous high-powered squad cars failed to restrain Agostino, 100 riot policemen in battle dress barely restrained the fans.

By the time the "moto-rodeo" – as Neapolitans have come to call Agostino's midnight madness was over, 21 people including eight policemen had been hurt in clashes and 12 Neapolitans were jailed.

Police said they suspect there is a method in Agostino's madness.

They believe he is part of a motorcycle gang of pickpockets who use him to distract the police while they go about their criminal business.

AP News Release

ZEEB
Alex Rode

Zeeb prowls
up alleys & down
late, when night like a broad dull cleaver
severs the town's main artery
& streetlamps exhale grime & pollen in yellow haloes
ubiquitous as death within the compound walls
he strikes impartially in the wan hours
a candid prophet
a hawker of reality

Zeeb & the night guards have a working agreement:
whatever moves in the southwest quadrant, where beggars & petty
vendors & other undesirables are housed, is his to violate & plunder
to butcher, mutilate, rob
or merely terrorize
while they, the olive-clad night elite
ferret out conspirators & thieves
in the more prosperous sectors

it is a mutually advantageous pact
preserving the stability of the State
the safety of its defenders
the crush of fear among the rabble
& Zeeb's solitary freedom

Zeeb, mute & amber-eyed
pensile bones visible through pitted hide
moves like a fog
seeking victims
kills for coin, food, rags, or the joy of snuffing out a lifebeat with
his fingers
he is neither cruel nor mad
he does unto others as he would have them do unto him
would concur in the categorical imperative had he been schooled in
formal ethics
obeys the laws
pay obeisance to the Church
& in his daylight dealings with other men
though somewhat distant & eccentric
is always impeccably correct

Zeeb is celibate, friendless, stable & pious
free of ambition, virtually free of doubt
ideal compound dweller
a perfect subject of the State

if he has even wondered about justice
the inviolability of human life
mercy, freedom, love or compassion
there is nothing in the world of sensible phenomena
to make him question his nocturnal acts

in his own uncomplicated way, he believes in God & Satan
in efficiency
competence
& unlike the others, in solitude
he views himself as a minor implement
in the struggle to educate the citizenry
a man fortunate to have found his secluded niche
within the communality of the compound

while others sleep
Zeeb toils at raw reality
at sunup, when the work brigades march to bunkers & weapon plants
he dreams exultantly of murder

Zeeb!

Wha . . . What is it?

The Captain wants to see you, right away!

The Captain?

Yes! Right now!

Zeeb dons his holiday grays & starched white blouse
fumbling

scraping shoe tips on his calves
brush-plowing through his hair
a reel of images flickering through his mind
as he attempts to visualize the lofty official

he has never met the Captain
nor Lieutenants, Sergeants, Corporals
his sole contact was with underlings
who, with a splatter of brown juice in the dirt, passed soggy &
  contemptuous commands
at dusk

now, in blatant sunlight
he scurries, limp-runs to the sandbagged Central Hall
is ushered by the clerks & ready gunners
through armoured doors
into the presence of the Chief

Zeeb trips on thick carpet pile, bows, sputters, cowers as the reedy gaze
behind the desk audits his worth from toe to crown

the Captain is young
his face seems to lack all history
but for a brown mole set into the hollow of his chin

So you are – Zeeb?
Zeeb, the night killer?

Yes, sir.

They tell me you derive a certain pleasure
from garroting strangers on deserted streets.

Well, it's a living, sir.

Just a vocation, then, old man?
You don't dote on your power, tingle a bit when your victims'
  flesh turns blue?
Don't you taste glory for an instant as life & soul flee with a gasp
  from the shell?

No, sir, not I.
It's just my job
& my duty.

the captain rises, frowning, mole drained of its purple ink
walks slowly to confront Zeeb's eyes
the gold medallion of the Church
blazing through the shirt's incision

Zeeb backs a step
pupils darting about the vastness of the room
empty but for the two of them
I'm not going to hurt you.
I only want the truth.
Perhaps you've never thought about this
quite like this before.

Yes, sir.

We're brothers, you know, you & I.
We share a great deal more
than the barriers between us sunder.
Is there nothing you feel at all
in the moment of decisive death?

Zeeb, still half-bent & palsied
reads the Captain's lineless cheeks
& grovels:

Fear, sir.
Fear is what I feel.
Fear.

suddenly, the pale official lips
twist to a sneer
the medal rattles on the uniform
& the Captain's open, slashing hand
lands on Zeeb's temple like a cudgel

Fear!
You'd rather be a tanner than a killer!
You'd rather dig among worms with a spade
than ply your night trade for the worms'
  morning meal?

I must confess I would, sir.

You must confess you would, sir!
I heard about your exploits, Zeeb!
your murderous cunning, stealth,
your loyalty & skill.
I heard how like a lightning-ray you struck
leaving your victims placid, unaware
child-mouthed as if they died at birth
degenerates & beggars
perishing in seeming innocence.
Only a coward or a God, I thought
would choose to murder in the blind of night
when no one but the stars would see the final gaze of living, knowing eyes.
You are no God.

That's right all right.

No, sir.

You'd like to be a bagger on the sand crews
or water boy, or mortar-mixer?
I won't give you the pleasure.
You'll go on being just a snail
feeding on gnats in the darkness.

the Captain laughed, dropped in the swivel chair
pressed a chord of buttons with his hand

Why, Zeeb, you're not even half a man!
the guards were through the door already
quick to seize the Captain's sneer
they had their coarse palms deep into the old man's skin

Wait! One last order, Zeeb
from these dizzying heights
before you crawl back to your burrow:
tonight, an enemy of the State, posing as a beggar in a tattered suit of grays
will come from some subterranean pit
in the southwest quadrant
seeking food & water.
Dispatch him with your coward's skill
we can't be bothered with such trifles.
before they kicked him down a score of steps

out of the Central Hall, into the blinding noonhour dust
he heard a guard yell:

You could've been a corporal, at the least!

Zeeb makes his way
arm up to ward off the sun & green diurnal flies
to the barracks, where, still trembling, he falls into a nightmarish sleep
dreaming, for once, not of murder
but of the oppressive cruelty of the sun

he wakes much later than usual
the moon is high above the barracks door
he can hear the breathing of the others in their cots
as he dresses, he feels the nightly surge of joy
but stifles it, angrily, almost at once

three hundred & eleven steps from the barracks door
he sees he sees a bent old hag
with a rent old bag
sliding along a building wall

there is no fire in his throat
Zeeb ignores her & goes on

He veers into an alley mouth
flexes his tired fingers
until his peaked ears pick the stillness out of silence
the muffled, padded soles on powder
the terse breath & bristling hairs
of an approaching figure

Zeeb leaps

elbow crook vised around the victim's throat
Zeeb grinds his biceps unto death
but this time
while the man's gun twirls to the ground
Zeeb twists his skull a full half turn
looks long & deep into the other's eyes
drinks profoundly of the final knowledge in those eyes
the last words heard by the murdered man
just before the golden medal was ripped by the chain from his flaccid neck:

Thank you, sir.
Thank you.

HEALING A LUNATIC BOY
Charles Causely

Trees turned and talked to me,
Tigers sang,
Houses put on leaves,
Water rang.
Flew in, flew out
On my tongue's thread
A speech of birds
From my hurt head.

At my fine lion
Fire and cloud kissed,
Rummaged the green bone
Beneath my wrist.
I saw a sentence
Of fern and tare
Write with loud light
The mineral air.

On a stopped morning
The city spoke,
In my rich mouth
Oceans broke.
No more on the spun shore
I walked unfed.
I drank the sweet sea,
Stones were bread.

Then came the healer
Grave as grass,
His hair of water
And hands of glass.
I watched at his tongue
The white words eat,
In death, dismounted
At his stabbed feet.

Now river is river
And tree is tree,
My house stands still
As the northern sea.
On my hundred of parables
I heard him pray,
Seize my smashed world,
Wrap it away.

Now the pebble is sour,
The birds beat high,
The fern is silent,
The river dry.
A seething summer
Burned to bone
Feeds at my mouth
But finds a stone.

HUNGER
Traditional
Translated from the Yoruba (Nigeria) by Ulli Beier

Hunger makes a person climb up to the ceiling
And hold on to the rafters
It makes a person lie down –
But not feel at rest.
It makes a person lie down –
Unable to stand
It makes a person lie down –
And count the rafters
When the Moslem is not hungry, he says:
We are forbidden to eat monkey.
When Ibrahim is hungry he eats a baboon!
When hunger beats the woman in the harem,
She will run out into the street in daytime.
One who is hungry does not care for taboos.
One who is hungry does not care for death.
One who is hungry will take
Out of the sacrifice money.
When death shuts the door,
Hunger will open it.
"I have filled my belly yesterday"
Does not concern hunger
There is no God like one's throat.
We have to sacrifice daily to it.

AFRICAN BEGGAR
Raymond Tong

Sprawled in the dust outside the Syrian store,
a target for small children, dogs and flies,
a heap of verminous rags and matted hair,
he watches us with cunning, reptile eyes,
his noseless, smallpoxed face creased in a sneer.

Sometimes he shows his yellow stumps of teeth
and whines for alms, perceiving that we bear
the curse of pity; a grotesque mask of death,
with hands like claws about his begging-bowl.

But often he is lying all alone
within the shadow of a crumbling wall,
lost in the trackless jungle of his pain,
clutching the pitiless red earth in vain
and whimpering like a stricken animal.

COUNTING THE MAD
Donald Justice

This one was put in a jacket,
This one was sent home,
This one was given bread and meat
But would eat none,
And this one cried No No No
All day long.

This one looked at the window
As though it were a wall,
This one saw things that were not there,
This one things that were,
And this one cried No No No
All day long.

This one thought himself a bird,
This one a dog,
And this one thought himself a man,
An ordinary man,
And cried and cried No No No No
All day long.

ANTICHRIST AS A CHILD

James Reaney

When Antichrist was a child
He caught himself tracing
The capital letter A
On a window sill
And wondered why
Because his name contained no A.
And as he crookedly stood
In his mother's flower-garden
He wondered why she looked so sadly
Out of an upstairs window at him.
He wondered why his father stared so
Whenever he saw his little son
Walking in his soot-colored suit.
He wondered why the flowers
And even the ugliest weeds
Avoided his fingers and his touch.
And when his shoes began to hurt
Because his feet were becoming hooves
He did not let on to anyone
For fear they would shoot him for a monster.
He wondered why he more and more
Dreamed of eclipses of the sun,
Of sunsets, ruined towns and zeppelins,
And especially inverted, upside down churches.

PETERBOROUGH, England (UPI) – Wings flapping wildly, the "Birdman of Peterborough" took to the air today – and wound up with only a bloody nose to show for his flight.

"I'm not dismayed, really I'm not," Walter Cornelius said after his bid to fly by leaping off a supermarket roof with wood and hardboard "wings" strapped to his arms ended in an emergency landing.

Waving the homemade wings, he leaped from the 30-foot-high roof, wobbled, and nose-dived into the Nene River.

Moments after impact Cornelius, 44, bobbed to the surface, blood flowing from his nose.

He was otherwise unhurt, but the wings were a shambles.

"It was a bit painful," he said later. "But I'll try again."

UPI News Release

GUBBINAL

Wallace Stevens

That strange flower, the sun,
Is just what you say.
Have it your way.

The world is ugly.
And the people are sad.

That tuft of jungle feathers,
That animal eye,
Is just what you say.

That savage of fire,
That seed,
Have it your way.

The world is ugly,
And the people are sad.

MIAMI, Fla. (AP) – A dog lover blaming the death of his traveling Irish wolfhound on an airline took a $6.60 axe and hacked 18 slashes in a $5 million jetliner to get "what they owe me."

Thomas William Brown, 38, a carpenter who said he blamed Eastern Airlines for the death of his two-year-old champion, Lost River, threw black paint at a Boeing 727 cockpit yesterday and slashed its underbelly before a crew member stopped him, the FBI said.

The airline estimated the damage at $100,000.

The dog died May 22 of what a veterinarian called a heat stroke shortly after returning to Miami from Dallas in the cargo hold of an Eastern jet.

Brown launched a lawsuit against Eastern. Eastern said it was not negligent and asked yesterday for dismissal of the lawsuit.

Authorities said Brown then bought an axe and walked up to the jet as it unloaded passengers at Miami International Airport. He hacked through the metal skin, cables and hydraulic lines before Second Officer Jim Broadman asked him what he was doing.

Mr. Broadman said Brown replied: "None of your business.... Well, I guess I've done $5,000 damage to that airplane and that's what they owe me."

"He worked that righthand side over pretty good," an Eastern spokesman said. Brown was charged with destruction of an aircraft and jailed under $100,000 bond.

AP News Release

PASSION

John Robert Colombo

The wind was wild that day.
It blew a rose my way.

I caught it with no sound
And dashed it to the ground.

But then as I had feared
A greenish stalk appeared.

And where the rose had bled
There grew a human head.

I looked – but turned away.
The wind was wild that day.

THEY AROSE

Paul Hiebert

They arose, three dead men,
Stiff and dank,
From the gloomy depths
Of a water tank;
And they bowed full soon
To the rising moon,
For the one was Bill,
And the other two, Hank.

I WANTED TO SMASH

Raymond Souster

I wanted to smash
something in their dull
so stupid faces,

but you reached down
with a certain smile,
put a flower in my hand.

CRAZY HORSE THE SIOUX

Jim Burns

Crazy Horse was a Sioux
so listen to this!
He fought the whites,
   (you know, Custer
   and all that).
Rosebud, Wolf Mountain,
and the Wagon Box,
he was at them all.
Finally, one day,
   Buffalo all gone,
   kids starving,
   young men dead,
he decided to seek a truce,
so he rode to the reservation.
   "Ok Crazy Horse, welcome.
   Sure we'll talk peace, just
   step into this small, dark
   iron room."
But Crazy Horse was no fool.
He was all Sioux
and he made a break.
Some reservation Indians
grabbed him
        and a soldier
bayoneted him in the guts.
Crazy Horse the Sioux
   should have stayed
   in the wilds.
It's safer.

"But white men, who live in straight lines and squares, do not believe as I do. With them it is rather everything or nothing. And because of their strange beliefs, they are very persistent. They will even fight at night or in bad weather. But they hate the fighting itself. Winning is all they care about, and if they can do that by scratching a pen across paper or saying something into the wind, they are much happier.

They will not be content now to come and take revenge upon us for the death of the formerly Long Hair, which they could easily do. Indeed, if we all return to the agencies, they probably would not kill anyone. For killing is part of living, but they hate life. They hate war. In the old days they tried to make peace between us and the Crow and Pawnee, and we all shook hands and did not fight for a while, but it made everybody sick and our women began to be insolent and we could not wear our fine clothes if we were at peace. So finally we rode to a Crow camp and I made a speech there. 'We used to like you when we hated you,' I told those Crow. 'Now that we are friends of yours, we dislike you a great deal!'

They said: 'We used to think you Cheyenne were pretty when we fought you. Now you look ugly like dogs.'

"So it was an emergency, and we had a big battle."

Thomas Berger : *Little Big Man*

INDIAN RESERVATION: CAUGHNAWAGA

A. M. Klein

Where are the braves, the faces like autumn fruit,
who stared at the child from the colored frontispiece?
And the monosyllabic chief who spoke with his throat? —
Where are the tribes, the feathered bestiaries? —
Rank Aesop's animals erect and red,
with fur on their names to make all live things kin, —
Chief Running Deer, Black Bear, Old Buffalo Head?

Childhood, that wished me Indian, hoped that
one afterschool I'd leave the classroom chalk,
the varnish smell, the watered dust of the street,
to join the clean outdoors and the Iroquois track.
Childhood; but always, — as on a calendar, —
there stood that chief, with arms akimbo, waiting
the runaway mascot paddling to his shore.

With what strange moccasin stealth that scene is changed!
With French names, without paint, in overalls,
their bronze, like their nobility expunged, —
the men. Beneath their alimentary shawls
sit like black tents their squaws; while for the tourist's
brown pennies scattered at the old church door,
the ragged papooses jump, and bite the dust.

Their past is sold in a shop: the beaded shoes,
the sweetgrass basket, the curio Indian,
burnt wood and gaudy cloth and inch-canoes —
trophies and scalpings for a traveller's den.
Sometimes, it's true, they dance, but for a bribe;
after a deal don the bedraggled feather
and welcome a white mayor to the tribe.

This is a grassy ghetto, and no home.
These are but fauna in a museum kept.
The better hunters have prevailed. The game,
losing its blood, now makes these grounds its crypt.
The animal pale, the shine of the fur is lost,
bleached are their living bones. About them watch
as through a mist, the pious prosperous ghosts.

EVENING IN THE SUBURBS
AFTER JACQUES PRÉVERT

Raymond Souster

Around six he arrives
from a hard day at the office
His dog greets him
his children greet him
even his wife greets him
He sits down
his wife sits down
his children sit down
even his dog sits down
and they eat supper
Then he lights his cigar
reads the evening paper
the sports page
the markets the comics
Gets up
goes into the garden
where he adjusts the sprinkler
turns the water on
sits down again
watching the drops
fall through the air
and goes to sleep
in the deck-chair
When he wakes up
it's dark outside
the sprinkler's off
He lights a cigar
and goes inside
the house is empty
the lights are out
then he remembers
his wife's at the church
his children next door
watching TV
even his dog's gone
He takes a beer
from the refrigerator
but the beer doesn't taste right
he sits down again
in his easy chair
picks up the paper
but his eyes are tired
he doesn't feel like reading
Still he feels like doing something
and he takes the paper
and rips it down the middle
he goes to the kitchen
and takes the beer bottle
and throws it through the window
his dog coming from the cellar
gets booted in the rear
Then he feels better
he feels good again
sits down in his chair
falls asleep like a child.

"Barbie," a twelve-inch plastic teen-ager, is the best-known and best-selling doll in history. Since its introduction in 1959, the Barbie doll population of the world has grown to 12,000,000 – more than the human population of Los Angeles or London or Paris. Little girls adore Barbie because she is highly realistic and eminently dress-upable. Mattel, Inc., makers of Barbie, also sells a complete wardrobe for her, including clothes for ordinary daytime wear, clothes for formal party wear, clothes for swimming and skiing.

Recently Mattel announced a new improved Barbie doll. The new version has a slimmer figure, "real" eyelashes, and a twist-and-turn waist that makes her more humanoid than ever. Moreover, Mattel announced that, for the first time, any young lady wishing to purchase a new Barbie would receive a trade-in allowance for her old one.

What Mattel did not announce was that by trading in her old doll for a technologically improved model, the little girl of today, citizen of tomorrow's super-industrial world, would learn a fundamental lesson about the new society; that man's relationships with things are increasingly temporary.

Fashionable boutiques and working-class clothing stores have sprouted whole departments devoted to gaily colored and imaginatively designed paper apparel. Fashion magazines display breathtakingly sumptuous gowns, coats, pajamas, even wedding dresses made of paper. The bride pictured in one of these wears a long white train of lace-like paper that, the caption writer notes, will make "great kitchen curtains" after the ceremony.

Alvin Toffler : *Future Shock*

A SUPERMARKET IN CALIFORNIA

Allen Ginsberg

What thoughts I have of you tonight, Walt Whitman, for I walked down the sidestreets under the trees with a headache self-conscious looking at the full moon.
In my hungry fatigue, and shopping for images, I went into the neon fruit supermarket, dreaming of your enumerations!
What peaches and what penumbras! Whole families shopping at night! Aisles full of husbands! Wives in the avocados, babies in the tomatoes! – and you, Garcia Lorca, what were you doing down by the watermelons?

I saw you, Walt Whitman, childless, lonely old grubber, poking among the meats in the refrigerator and eyeing the grocery boys.
I heard you asking questions of each: Who killed the pork chops? What price bananas? Are you my Angel?
I wandered in and out of the brilliant stacks of cans following you, and followed in my imagination by the store detective.
We strode down the open corridors together in our solitary fancy tasting artichokes, possessing every frozen delicacy, and never passing the cashier.

Where are we going, Walt Whitman? The doors close in an hour. Which way does your beard point tonight?
(I touch your book and dream of our odyssey in the supermarket and feel absurd.)
Will we walk all night through solitary streets? The trees add shade to shade, lights out in the houses, we'll both be lonely.
Will we stroll dreaming of the lost America of love past blue automobiles in driveways, home to our silent cottage?
Ah, dear father, graybeard, lonely old courage-teacher, what America did you have when Charon quit poling his ferry and you got out on a smoking bank and stood watching the boat disappear on the black waters of Lethe?

STATUS SYMBOL

Mari Evans

   i
Have Arrived

   i
  am the
New Negro

   i
am the result of
President Lincoln
World War I
and Paris
the
Red Ball Express
white drinking fountains
sitdowns and
sit-ins
Federal Troops
Marches on Washington
    and
prayer meetings
today
They hired me
it
is a status
job . . .
along
with my papers
They
gave me my
Status Symbol

the
key
to the
White . . Locked . .
John

THE BALLAD OF MALCOLM X

Robert Leach

Malcolm X was a violent man,
Hated by the respected Ku Klux Klan:
His dad was sliced up on a railroad track
For the very good reason that he was black.
    . . .

Malcolm X, Malcolm's black,
Malcolm X, Malcolm's dead,
Shot from the front through to the back,
Shot through the belly and shot through the head.
    . . .

Malcolm X was a clever git:
When he got out of jail he did a flit,
And he wasn't seen again till he was a preacher-man,
Shouting "Respect!" for the dirty nigger-man.

Malcolm X, Malcolm's black,
Malcolm X, Malcolm's dead,
Shot from the front through to the back,
Shot through the belly and shot through the head.

Malcolm X was a bearded crab,
Scruffy and dirty – an American scab,
'Cause he never seemed frightened about what to say
Of the hypocritical platitudes of J. F. K.

Malcolm X was a dangerous guy,
The black man who above all must die,
'Cause he wouldn't give the white man his longed-for boost
And saw that the chickens were coming home to roost.

Malcolm X, Malcolm's black,
Malcolm X, Malcolm's dead,
Shot from the front through to the back,
Shot through the belly and shot through the head.

Malcolm X was a wicked man,
And must have been soft in his black brainpan
'Cause he wanted the nigger to be really free
In the great society of Lyndon B.

Malcolm X, Malcolm's black,
Malcolm X, Malcolm's dead,
Shot from the front through to the back,
Shot through the belly and shot through the head.

White kiddies won't be frightened when they're tucked up
   in bed
'Cause black ogre Malcolm is good and dead;
They'll go back to sleep when they wake up in the night
'Cause black ogre Malcolm can't give them a fright.

Malcolm X said what he thought,
Malcolm X did what he taught,
Malcolm X got what he bought –
The black mouse in the white trap beautifully caught:

    White men snort
    But they'll be taught,
'Cause Malcolm X didn't die for nought!

GAZING AT FALLING PETALS

Kubutsu
Translated by Harry Behn

Gazing at falling
petals, a baby almost
Looks like a Buddha

DELICATE JOHN

Brian Patten

Delicate John has moved away.
Listen to what the children said:

He couldn't make love
And he couldn't make money,
He had a gammy leg
(which they thought was funny).

Now John, tender and quiet as a habit,
is leading half a life among his books.
He cannot return from where he came
Because the children learnt

Of what they thought a lack of love,
Of his lack of money,
Of something unfamiliar in his brain
(which they thought was funny)

He sits at a window and sometimes they pass,
The children who gave him a monkey for his back,
They pass in twos they pass in threes,
They look contented and they look pleased.
John sits, he rots away,
Behind a lace curtain where he quietly cries
Tears as big as a choir boy's eyes.

What have they done to John,
What have they done to him?
The children who grow old,
Who squabble and grow thin,
Who lick their lips at disaster
And quietly whisper of sin.

STUPID

Graham Thomas

On the scrubbed front step
the milk bottles stand
sucked dry by hordes
of marauding birds.

And out in the garden
the prize blooms bend
unable to bear
the weight of cats;

But the police are seeking
a silent stranger
who likes his milk
and is jealous of flowers.

THE LITTLE MAN WITH WOODEN HAIR

Kenneth Patchen

There was a little man with wooden hair
Who'd sneak into the rear of busses
And holler, "Somebody just ate my mother!"
For that way, of course, he could count on a quick trim
Without having to pay for the broken window.

FAIRFAX, Va. (UPI) – A hatchet-wielding man dressed in a white bunny suit with floppy ears is creating consternation among Fairfax county police authorities. He now has struck twice in two weeks.

A security guard at a new housing development under construction in this Washington, D.C., suburb told police that he came upon the man whacking away at a porch post of one of the unfinished houses Thursday night.

When the guard approached, he said the Alice-in-Wonderland figure warned: "You are trespassing. If you come any closer, I'll chop off your head."

Whereupon the menacing bunny hippity-hopped off into a nearby woods.

UPI News Release

SILLYSUIT

Pete Morgan

This is a sillysuit I wear
an elbow through
the seat threadbare
and I don't know where
I'll wear it
again.

I wore it to the Palace
when they told me that the Queen
was hiding in the ivy
somewhere inbetween
the East Wing & the West Wing.

I wore it to the Castle
when they handed out the arms
and I heard the choristers
singing the psalms –
up to their thighs in ammunition.

I wore it to the Chapel
where the men were on their knees
praying to whatever gods
and all saying please –
as blue as their eyes the salvation.

I wore it to the brewery
I wore it to the fair
I wore it to make love in
& I wore it everywhere.

So Stitch & Snippit tailorman
cut another suit
sew it in the latest style
and let the trumpets toot
there is one reveille
I won't answer.

This is a billet-doux I bear
signed by Her Majesty
and that's quite rare
but I don't have a care
to wear that
again.

NORMAN MORRISON

Adrian Mitchell

On November 2nd 1965
in the multi-coloured multi-minded
United beautiful States of terrible America
Norman Morrison set himself on fire
outside the Pentagon
He was thirty-one, he was a Quaker,
and his wife (seen weeping in the newsreels)
and his three children
survive him as best they can.
He did it in Washington where everyone could see.
because
people were being set on fire
in the dark corners of Vietnam where nobody could see.
Their names, ages, beliefs and loves
are not recorded.
This is what Norman Morrison did.
He poured petrol over himself.
He burned. He suffered.
He died.
This is what he did
in the white heart of Washington
Where everyone could see.
He simply burned away his clothes,
his passport, his pink-tinted skin,
put on a new skin of flame
and became
Vietnamese.

We are not able even to *think* adequately about the behaviour that is at the annihilating edge. But what we think is less than what we know: what we know is less than what we love: what we love is so much less than what there is. And to that precise extent we are so much less than what we are.

R. D. Laing : *The Politics of Experience*

The buzz-saw snarled and rattled in the yard
And made dust and dropped stove-length sticks of wood,
Sweet-scented stuff when the breeze drew across it.
And from there those that lifted eyes could count
Five mountain ranges one behind the other
Under the sunset far into Vermont.
And the saw snarled and rattled, snarled and rattled,
As it ran light, or had to bear a load.
And nothing happened: day was all but done.
Call it a day, I wish they might have said
To please the boy by giving him the half hour
That a boy counts so much when saved from work.
His sister stood beside them in her apron
To tell them "Supper". At the word, the saw,
Neither refused the meeting, But the hand!
The boy's first outcry was a rueful laugh,
As he swung toward them holding up the hand
Half in appeal, but half as if to keep
The life from spilling. Then the boy saw all —
Since he was old enough to know, big boy
Doing a man's work, though a child at heart —
He saw all spoiled. "Don't let him cut my hand off —
The Doctor, when he comes. Don't let him, sister!"
So. But the hand was gone already.
The doctor put him in the dark of ether.
He lay and puffed his lips out with his breath.
And then — the watcher at his pulse took fright.
No one believed. They listened at his heart.
Little – less – nothing! and that ended it.
No more to build on there. And they, since they
Were not the one dead, turned to their affairs.

"OUT, OUT"

ROBERT FROST

"For gold that is gone,"
Said the girl,
" I weep distractedly."

I turned to the youth,
"And you?"
"For what I have not gained,"
he cried,
"Possessing her
I lost myself and died."

And so we sat, a trio
Tuned to sobs,
And miles to go
And miles and miles apart

Till they, amazed
That one as old as I
Had juice enough for tears,
Dried their streaming eyes
To ask the cause of mine.

I told of the grit I'd found
In a grain of truth,
Mentioned an aching tooth
Decayed with fears
And the sum of all I'd lost
In the increased tax on years.

They yawned and rose
And walked away. I moved
To go but death sat down.
His cunning hand
Explored my skeleton.

Anne Wilkinson

On a bench in a park
Where I went walking,
A boy and girl,
Their new hearts breaking
Sat side by side
And miles apart
And they wept most bitterly.

"Why do you mourn,"
I asked,
"You, who are barely born?"

ON A BENCH IN A PARK

LADY LAZARUS
Sylvia Plath

I have done it again.
One year in every ten
I manage it —

A sort of walking miracle, my skin
Bright as a Nazi lampshade,
My right foot

A paperweight
My face a featureless, fine
Jew linen.

Peel off the napkin
O my enemy.
Do I terrify? —

The nose, the eye pits, the full set of teeth?
The sour breath
Will vanish in a day.

Soon, soon the flesh
The grave cave ate will be
At home on me

And I a smiling woman,
I am only thirty.
And like the cat I have nine times to die.

This is Number Three
What a trash
To annihilate each decade.

What a million filaments.
The peanut-crunching crowd
Shoves in to see

Them unwrap me hand and foot —
The big strip tease.
Gentlemen, ladies

These are my hands
My knees,
I may be skin and bone,

Nevertheless, I am the same, identical woman.
The first time it happened I was ten.
It was an accident.

The second time I meant
To last it out and not come back at all.
I rocked shut

As a seashell.
They had to call and call
And pick the worms off me like sticky pearls.

Dying
Is an art, like everything else.
I do it exceptionally well.

I do it so it feels like hell.
I do it so it feels real.
I guess you could say I've a call.

It's easy enough to do it in a cell.
It's easy enough to do it and stay put.
It's the theatrical

Comeback in broad day
To the same place, the same face, the same brute
Amused shout:

"A miracle!"
That knocks me out.
There is a charge

For the eyeing of my scars, there is a charge
For the hearing of my heart —
It really goes.

And there is a charge, a very large charge
For a word or a touch
Or a bit of blood

Or a piece of my hair or my clothes.
So, so Herr Doktor.
So, Herr Enemy.

I am your opus,
I am your valuable,
The pure gold baby

That melts to a shriek.
I turn and burn.
Do not think I underestimate your great concern.

Ash, ash —
You poke and stir.
Flesh, bone, there is nothing there —

A cake of soap,
A wedding ring,
A gold filling.

Herr God, Herr Lucifer
Beware.
Beware.

Out of the ash
I rise with my red hair
And I eat men like air.

THE BULL MOOSE

Alden Nowlan

Down from the purple mist of trees on the mountain,
lurching through forests of white spruce and cedar,
stumbling through tamarack swamps,
came the bull moose
to be stopped at last by a pole-fenced pasture.

Too tired to turn or, perhaps, aware
there was no place left to go, he stood with the cattle.
They, scenting the musk of death, seeing his great head
like the ritual mask of a blood god, moved to the other end
of the field, and waited.

The neighbours heard of it, and by afternoon
cars lined the road. The children teased him
with alder switches and he gazed at them
like an old, tolerant collie. The women asked
if he could have escaped from a Fair.

The oldest man in the parish remembered seeing
a gelded moose yoked with an ox for plowing.
The young men snickered and tried to pour beer
down his throat, while their girl friends took their pictures.

And the bull moose let them stroke his tick-ravaged flanks,
let them pry open his jaws with bottles, let a giggling girl
plant a purple cap
of thistles on his head.

When the wardens came, everyone agreed it was a shame
to shoot anything so shaggy and cuddlesome.
He looked like the kind of pet
women put to bed with their sons.

So they held their fire. But just as the sun dropped in the river
the bull moose gathered his strength
like a scaffolded king, straightened and lifted his horns
so that even the wardens backed away as they raised their rifles.
When he roared, people ran to their cars. All the young men
leaned on their automobile horns as he toppled.

MAN WITH ONE SMALL HAND

P. K. Page

One hand is smaller than the other. It
must always be loved a little like a child;
requires attention constantly, implies
it needs his frequent glance to nurture it.

He holds it sometimes with the larger one
as adults lead a child across a street.
Finding it his and suddenly alien
rallies his interest and his sympathy.

Sometimes you come upon him unawares
just quietly staring at it where it lies
as mute and somehow perfect as a flower.

But no. It is not perfect. He admits
it has its faults : it is not strong or quick.
At night it vanishes to reappear
in dreams full-size, lost or surrealist.

Yet has its place like memory or a dog –
is never completely out of mind – a rod
to measure all uncertainties against.

Perhaps he loves it too much, sets too much stock
simply in its existence. Ah, but look!
It has its magic. See how it will fit
so sweetly, sweetly in the infant's glove.

VULTURE

Douglas Livingstone

On ragged black sails
he soars hovering over
everything and death;
a blight in the eye
of the stunning sun.

An acquisitive droop
of beak, head and neck
dangles, dully angling,
a sentient pendulum
next to his keeled chest.

His eyes peer, piously
bloodless and hooded,
far-sighted, blighting
grasses, trees, hill-passes,
stones, streams, bones – ah, bones –

with the tacky slack
of flesh adherent.
A slow ritual fold
of candid devil's palms
in blasphemous prayer –

the still wings sweep closed –
the hyaena of skies
plummets from the pulpit
of a tall boredom
swallowing as he falls.

He brakes lazily
before his back breaks
to settle on two
creaky final wing-beats
flinging twin dust-winds.

He squats once fearfully.
Flushed with unhealthy plush
and pregustatory
satisfaction, head back,
he jumps lumpishly up.

Slack neck with the pecked
skin thinly shaking, he
sidles aside then stumps
his deliberate banker's
gait to the stinking meal.

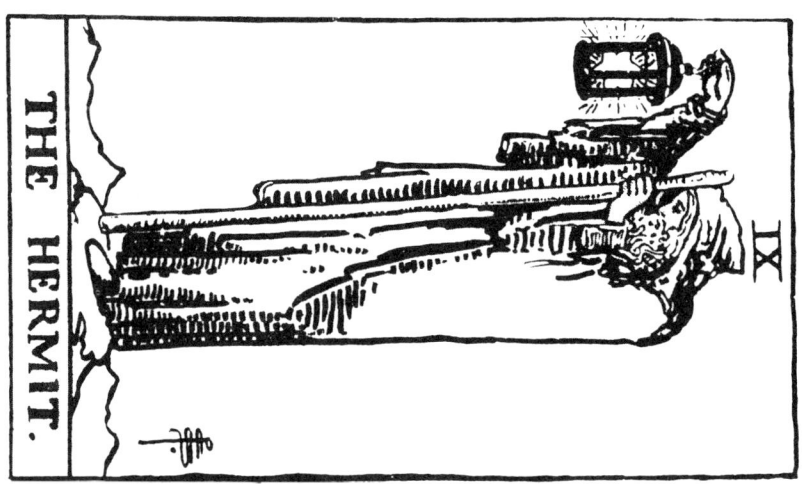

We are shattered, tattered, demented remnants of a once-glorious army. Among us are Princes, and Captains of Armies, Lords of Battles, amnesic, aphasic, ataxic, jerkily trying to recall what was the battle the sounds of which still ring in our ears – is the battle still raging? If we could only make contact with Headquarters, only make our way back to join the main body of the Army. . . .

R. D. Laing : *The Politics of Experience*

"How do I love thee?
Let me count the ways."

Or say . . . I love you . . .
How many ways can you say it?
Or does saying it matter?
How about doing, being?
"All you need is love."
"Love makes the world go round."
Love, honour, and obey.
The love that passes all understanding.
It is a rare person, poet or not, who
has not tried some time to express
something so personal and immediate
as love. But words do not seem
to be enough.

Actions speak louder than words.

Familial . . . .
Romantic . . . .
Brotherly . . . .
Sexual . . . .
Platonic . . . .
Holy . . . .
Profane . . . .
Motherly . . . .
Puppy . . . .
Patriotic . . . .
Selfish . . . .
Generous . . . .
Unrequited . . . .

Love conquers all

AMOR VINCIT OMNIA

ELVIRA MADIGAN

William Dick

Jerkily but surely one by one
he robbed his brilliant uniform
of brass buttons, which like severed
eyes fell blinking in the sun.

Off too a penknife hacked the splendid
gold brocade and the proud emblems
of a regiment's straitlaced years. Alarmed,
she watched beside him
              in the grass, surrounded
by the low monotonous dirge of bees,
the swift uncertain glint of butterflies.

A scarecrow's civilian coat restored
another self; no more for her
the circus tights, but a circling gown.
The world with all its frantic horde

contracted into two, where stood revealed
each other's awesome universe.
Face to face they moved through time;
flaked in sunlight she danced
              in the rippling field
to the low monotonous dirge of bees,
the swift uncertain glint of butterflies.

The carnival played on without its star
(instead she teetered secretly
on clothesline taut above the poppies),
and the guards paraded as before.

The children ask, but mother speaks
no more of him, and looks away.
They crush in their mouths the purple flesh
of berries while white cream
              drips down their cheeks,
by the low monotonous dirge of bees,
the swift uncertain glint of butterflies.

They scrape for roots and fungi in the wild
when the vanished world refuses bread.
What will truly consummate
this love, indifferently sealed

in the toils of iron circumstance?
The surest frame for love is death.
A pistol shot – and life's caught still;
still forever is her careless dance
to the low monotonous dirge of bees,
the swift uncertain glint of butterflies.

SUZANNE WEARS A LEATHER COAT

Leonard Cohen

Suzanne wears a leather coat.
Her legs are insured by many burnt bridges.
Her calves are full as spinnakers
in a clean race, hard from following music
beyond the maps of any audience.

Suzanne wears a leather coat
because she is not a civilian.
She never walks casually down Ste Catherine
because with every step she must redeem
the clubfoot crowds and stalk the field
of huge hail-stones that never melted,
I mean the cemetery.

Stand up! stand!
Suzanne is walking by.
She wears a leather coat. She won't stop
to bandage the fractures she walks between.
She must not stop, she must not
carry money.
Many are the workers in charity.

Few serve the lilac,
few heal with mist.
Suzanne wears a leather coat.
Her breasts yearn for marble.
The traffic halts: people fall out
of their cars. None of their most drooling
thoughts are wild enough
to build the ant-full crystal city
she would splinter with the tone of her step.

EXPLANATIONS OF LOVE

Carl Sandburg

There is a place where love begins and a place where love ends.

There is a touch of two hands that foils all dictionaries.

There is a look of eyes fierce as a big Bethlehem open hearth furnace or a little green-fire acetylene torch.

There are single careless bywords portentous as a big bend in the Mississippi River.

Hands, eyes, bywords – out of these love makes battlegrounds and workshops.

There is a pair of shoes love wears and the coming is a mystery.

There is a warning love sends and the cost of it is never written till long afterward.

There are explanations of love in all languages and not one found wiser than this:

There is a place where love begins and a place where love ends – and love asks nothing.

... they on the other hand wonder greatly at the folly of all other nations, which in buying a colt, where a little money is at stake, are so chary and circumspect, that though he be almost all bare, yet they will not buy him unless the saddle and all the harness are taken off, lest under those coverings is hid some gall or sore. And yet in choosing a wife, who shall be either pleasure or trouble to them all their life after, they are so reckless that while all the rest of the woman's body is covered with clothes, they judge her by scarcely one hand-breadth (for they can see no more than her face), and so join her to them not without great peril of evil agreeing together, if anything in her body afterward offend and displease them.

                            Thomas More : *Utopia*

THE GARDEN OF THE SEXES

Jay MacPherson

I have a garden closed away
And shadowed from the light of day
Where Love hangs bound on every tree
And I alone go free.

His sighs, that turn the weathers round,
His tears, that water all the ground
His blood, that reddens in the vine,
These all are mine.

At night the golden apple-tree
Is my fixed station, whence I see
Terrible, sublime and free,
My loves go wheeling over me.

A SLICE OF WEDDING CAKE

Robert Graves

Why have such scores of lovely, gifted girls
    Married impossible men?
Simple self-sacrifice may be ruled out,
    And missionary endeavour, nine times out of ten.

Repeat "impossible men": not merely rustic,
    Foul-tempered or depraved
(Dramatic foils chosen to show the world
    How well women behave, and always have behaved).

Impossible men: idle, illiterate,
    Self-pitying, dirty, sly,
For whose appearance even in City parks
    Excuses must be made to casual passers-by.

Has God's supply of tolerable husbands
    Fallen, in fact, so low?
Or do I always over-value woman
    At the expense of man?
                Do I?
                It might be so.

FOR HETTIE

Leroi Jones

My wife is left-handed.
which implies a fierce de-
termination. A complete other
worldliness. IT'S WEIRD, BABY.
The way some folks
are always trying to be
different. A sin & a shame.
But then, she's been a bohemian
all of her life . . . black stockings
refusing to take orders. I sit
patiently, trying to tell her
whats right. TAKE THAT DAMN
PENCIL OUTTA THAT HAND. YOU'RE
RITING BACKWARDS. & such. but
to no avail. & it shows
in her work. Left-handed coffee,
Left-handed eggs; when she comes
in at night . . . it's her left hand
offered for me to kiss. Damn.
& now her belly droops over the seat.
They say it's a child. But
I ain't quite so sure.

PSYCHE WITH THE CANDLE

Archibald MacLeish

Love which is the most difficult mystery
Asking from every young one answers
And most from those most eager and most beautiful –
Love is a bird in a fist:
To hold it hides it, to look at it lets it go.
It will twist loose if you lift so much as a finger.
It will stay if you cover it – stay but unknown and invisible.
Either you keep it forever with fist closed
Or let it fling
Singing in fervor of sun and in song vanish.
There is no answer other to this mystery.

ADOLESCENCE

P. K. Page

In love they wore themselves in a green embrace.
A silken rain fell through the spring upon them.
In the park she fed the swans and he
whittled nervously with his strange hands.
And white was mixed with all their colours
as if they drew it from the flowering trees.

At night his two-finger whistle brought her down
the waterfall stairs to his shy smile
which, like an eddy, turned her round and round
lazily and slowly so her will
was nowhere – as in dreams things are and aren't.

Walking along the avenues in the dark
street lamps sang like sopranos in their heads
with a violence they never understood
and all their movements when they were together
had no conclusion.

Only leaning into the question had they motion:
after they parted were savage and swift as gulls.
Asking and asking the hostile emptiness
they were as sharp as partly sculptured stone
and all who watched, forgetting, were amazed
to see them form and fade before their eyes.

Compassion, not unlike love, abolishes the distance, the inbetween which always exists in human intercourse, and if virtue will always be ready to assert that it is better to suffer wrong than to do wrong, compassion will transcend this by stating in complete and even naive sincerity that it is easier to suffer than to see others suffer.

Hannah Arendt : *On Revolution*

FALL OF THE EVENING STAR

Kenneth Patchen

Speak softly; sun going down
Out of sight. Come near me now.

Dear dying fall of wings as birds
Complain against the gathering dark ...

Exaggerate the green blood in grass;
The music of leaves scraping space;

Multiply the stillness by one sound;
By one syllable of your name ...

And all that is little is soon giant,
All that is rare grows in common beauty

To rest with my mouth on your mouth
As somewhere a stars falls

And the earth takes it softly, in natural love ...
Exactly as we take each other ... and go to sleep.

COLOURS

Yevgeny Yevtushenko

When your face
appeared over my crumpled life
at first I understood
only the poverty of what I have.
Then its particular light
on woods, on rivers, on the sea,
became my beginning in the coloured world
in which I had not yet had my beginning.
I am so frightened, I am so frightened,
of the unexpected sunrise finishing,
of revelations
and tears and the excitement finishing.
I don't fight it, my love is this fear,
I nourish it who can nourish nothing,
love's slipshod watchman.
Fear hems me in.
I am conscious that these minutes are short
and that the colours in my eyes will vanish
when your face sets.

The other path to knowing "the secret" is love. Love is active penetration of the other person, in which my desire to know is stilled by union. In the act of fusion I know you, I know myself, I know everybody – and I "know" nothing.

Erich Fromm : *The Art of Loving*

FOUR LOVE POEMS AFTER READING THE CHINESE

Henry Graham

1.
This morning the sky is so leaden.
Catching sight of a seagull
through misted glass brings tears
to my eyes. And later
in the grey rain wet streets
the sight of a girl with
short hair stops me in my tracks.
I know that when I eventually
meet you, you will be cold to me,
and show me again the ring
given to you by another.

2.
When I hear that you have been
asking for me, even days
after, I look for you.
It is approaching the time of the
full moon and the tides are high.
The sound of your name releases
a flood of remembering.

THE REMAINS

Mark Strand

I empty myself of the names of others.
I empty my pockets. I empty my shoes and leave them beside the road. At night I turn back the clocks; I open the family album and look at myself as a boy.

What good does it do? The hours have done their job.
I say my own name. I say goodbye.
The words follow each other downwind.
I love my wife but send her away.

My parents rise out of their thrones
into the milky rooms of clouds. How can I sing?
Time tells me what I am. I change and I am the same.
I empty myself of my life and my life remains.

A VALEDICTION FORBIDDING MOURNING

John Donne

As virtuous men pass mildly away,
    And whisper to their souls to go,
Whilst some of their sad friends do say,
    The breath goes now, and some say, No:

So let us melt, and make no noise,
    No tear-floods, nor sigh-tempests move;
'Twere profanation of our joys
    To tell the laity our love.

Moving of th' earth brings harms and fears,
    Men reckon what it did, and meant;
But trepidation of the spheres,
    Though greater far, is innocent.

Dull sublunary lovers' love
    (Whose soul is sense) cannot admit
Absence, because it doth remove
    Those things which elemented it.

But we by a love so much refined
    That ourselves know not what it is,
Inter-assurèd of the mind,
    Care less eyes, lips and hands to miss.

Our two souls therefore, which are one,
    Though I must go, endure not yet
A breach, but an expansion,
    Like gold to airy thinness beat.

If they be two, they are two so
    As stiff twin compasses are two;
Thy soul, the fix'd foot, makes no show
    To move, but doth, if th' other do.

And though it in the centre sit,
    Yet, when the other far doth roam,
It leans, and hearkens after it,
    And grows erect, as that comes home.

Such wilt thou be to me, who must,
    Like th' other foot, obliquely run;
Thy firmness makes my circle just,
    And makes me end where I begun.

MAG

Carl Sandburg

I wish to God I never saw you, Mag.
I wish you never quit your job and came along with me.
I wish we never bought a licence and a white dress
For you to get married in the day we ran off to a minister
And told him we would love each other and take care of each other
Always and always long as the sun and the rain lasts anywhere.
Yes, I'm wishing now you lived somewhere away from here
And I was a bum on the bumpers a thousand miles away dead broke
I wish the kids had never come
And rent and coal and clothes to pay for
And a grocery man calling for cash,
Every day cash for beans and prunes.
I wish to God I never saw you, Mag.
I wish to God the kids had never come.

AS THE MIST LEAVES NO SCAR

Leonard Cohen

As the mist leaves no scar
On the dark green hill,
So my body leaves no scar
On you, nor ever will.

When wind and hawk encounter,
What remains to keep?
So you and I encounter,
Then turn, then fall to sleep.

As many nights endure
Without a moon or star,
So will we endure
When one is gone and far.

The experience of separateness arouses anxiety; it is, indeed, the source of all anxiety. Being separate means being cut off, without any capacity to use my human powers. Hence to be separate means to be helpless, unable to grasp the world – things and people – actively; it means that the world can invade me without my ability to react.

Erich Fromm : The Art of Loving

JACKIE'S ONE-SHOT

Stanley Cooperman

Because
I am no leaf of love
to be cut and mounted
in the coffin of your
smile,

Because
I am more than oddness,
titillation of a vein
or specimen
of sudden ripening,

I give back your apple.
Let it rot
behind your teeth
if you have numbered
any part of me.

Single-entry, was it?
then the page
is blank,
and you have divided
       nothing
between the covers
of your skin
but a reed of dust:

a puff of last week's
wind.

I went to the Garden of Love,
And saw what I never had see:
A Chapel was built in the midst,
Where I used to play on the green.

And the gates of this Chapel were shut,
And "Thou shalt not" writ over the door;
So I turn'd to the Garden of Love
That so many sweet flowers bore;

And I saw it was filled with graves,
And tomb-stones where flowers should be;
And Priests in black gowns were walking their rounds,
And binding with briars my joys & desires.

William Blake : "Garden of Love"

All tragedies are finished by a death,
  All comedies are ended by a marriage;
The future states of both are left to faith.

Lord Byron : "Don Juan"

FOUR POEMS AFTER READING THE CHINESE

Henry Graham

3.
Tonight I am drinking. The beer
is good, and the faces are all filled
with teeth: we all enjoy
the bright lights and the laughter.
Even I am laughing, though
the girl I am with asks
why I am so bitter.

4.
I am depressed by the cold weather.
I know the winter will be
over soon, and I have not much
to say. Writing these words
is more like touching your arm.

CANADIAN LOVE SONG

Alden Nowlan

Your Body's a small word with many meanings.
Love. If. Yes. But. Death.
Surely I will love you a little while,
perhaps as long as I have breath.

December is thirteen months long.
July's one afternoon; therefore
lovers must outwit wool,
learn how to puncture fur.

To my love's bed, to keep her warm,
I'll carry wrapped and heated stones.
That which is comfort to the flesh
is sometimes torture to the bones.

YOU HELD OUT THE LIGHT

Gwendolyn MacEwen

You held out the light to light my cigarette
But when I leaned down to the flame
It singed my eyebrows and my hair;
Now it is always the same – no matter where
We meet, you burn me.
I must always stop and rub my eyes
And beat the living fire from my hair.

THE TAXI

Amy Lowell

When I go away from you
The world beats dead
Like a slackened drum.
I call out for you against the jutted stars
And shout into the ridges of the wind.
Streets coming fast,
One after the other,
Wedge you away from me,
And the lamps of the city prick my eyes
So that I can no longer see your face.
Why should I leave you,
To wound myself upon the sharp edges of the night?

FIRE GARDENS

Gwendolyn MacEwen

We sped through galaxies like burning gardens
and long-travelling light linked your eye
with mine, there in the hollow part of time.
As beams unbroken, our light years
outdistanced our dark, and many sun-flowers
burst our dreams, and there were
aliens moons that orbited the heart.

Somehow the continents of night were sinking
and the huge wild gardens disappeared.
Love, we endured love as the night endured
its suns and stars, and finally far blackness
was the meaning of our light.
And O, we had meant forever to rewrite
the mathematics of a thousand worlds
and chase escaping suns
down fiery paths of night.

But a collision of love stole time and breath
in a garden whose flowers were flames
which burned beyond death.

IN FORMER DAYS

Anonymous   Translated from the
Sanskrit by John Brough

In former days we'd both agree
That you were me, and I was you.
What has now happened to us two,
That you are you, and I am me?

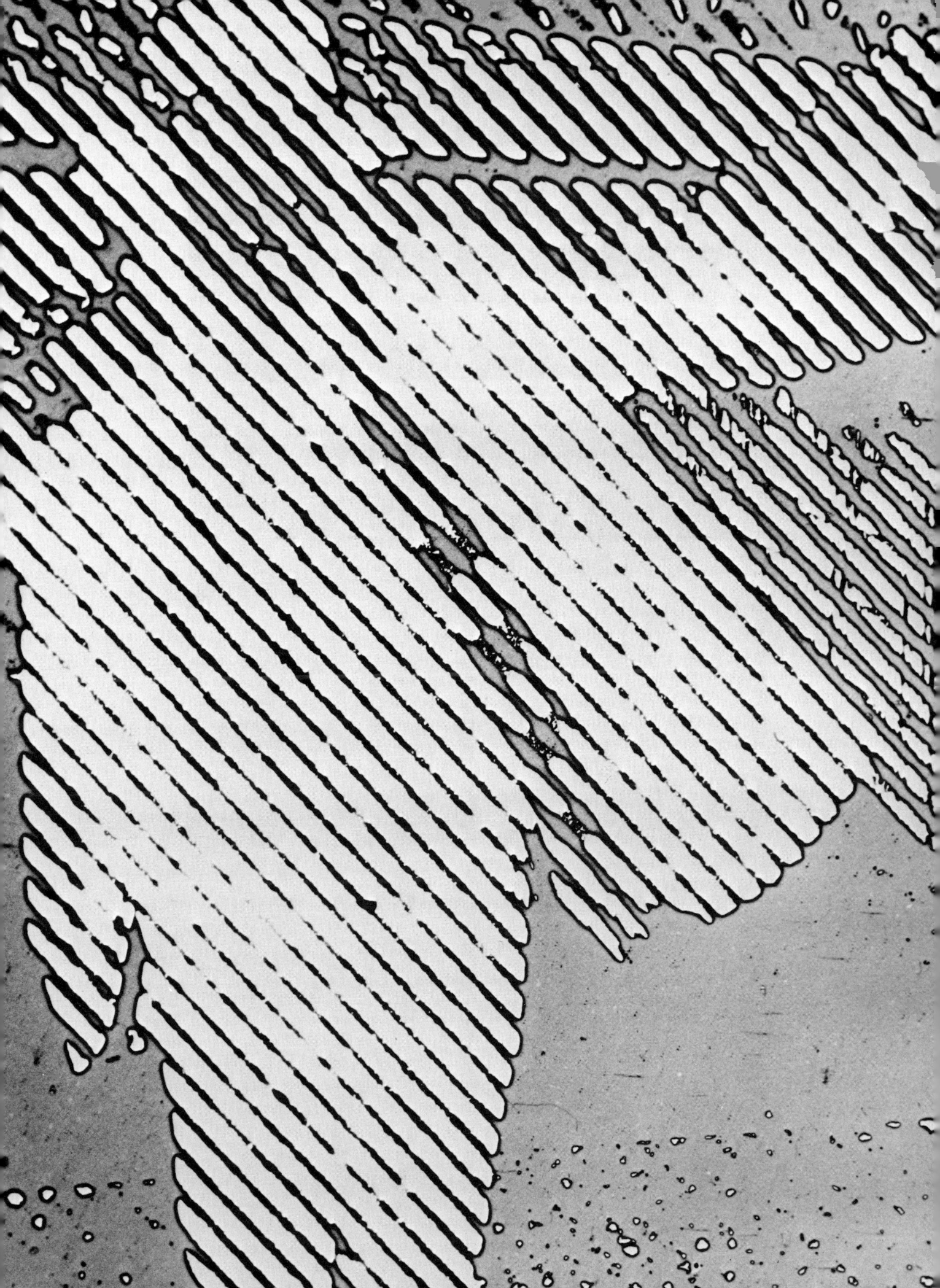

> For I looked into the future
> Far as human eye could see
> Saw a vision of the world
> And all the wonders that would be

Will they be? Alfred, Lord Tennyson wrote of the future in "Locksley Hall" in the last century. He saw airships, travel and commerce, and he saw battles and, finally, universal peace. He didn't see spreading, piling, garbage, automated factories, footsteps on the moon, mushroom clouds . . . .

He saw and he didn't see.

As you see on the following pages, Olaf Stapledon charted a vision of life to the end of time. He did not see the Second World War, and individual lives.

He saw and he didn't see.

And so it goes. But if there is any one kind of man who can see more clearly, it is the artist, the poet. He has something of the prophet in him. And though his single moments of vision may not offer so very much, they all add up, and so do those of other poets.

So we have gathered some moments of insight together; visions of the future, visions of how it is to experience someone else's sensations of being alive, visions of change and becoming. All these poems share

A GIFT OF PROPHECY

TO THE POETS OF THE SEVENTIES

Robert Conrad

we are the children
coming into our own
turning from the old ways
to a decade of possibilities
flower. harp. nuclear fire
pyramid. the edges run

so small and weak they are
so preciously tender in
our hands that they
will run like sand through
the fingers hold them close
or they will slide away

our hands may shake
but the first is grown huge
the braincomb multiplied
and no difference in essence
no less pitiless to wield
the thunderbolt over the
cabins of the poor over the barren lands

and on the rim of a vortex:
who would look at the stars?
except the fortunate ones
except maybe the survivors
the tree in my ear is scorched
with concepts the masks
have blinded me let us make
a new thing for ourselves
let us stand watch
over the coming years

THE WARNING

Adelaide Crapsey

Just now,
Out of the strange
Still dusk . . . as strange, as still . . .
A white moth flew. Why am I grown
So cold?

PROGRESSION OF THE SPECIES

Brian Aldiss

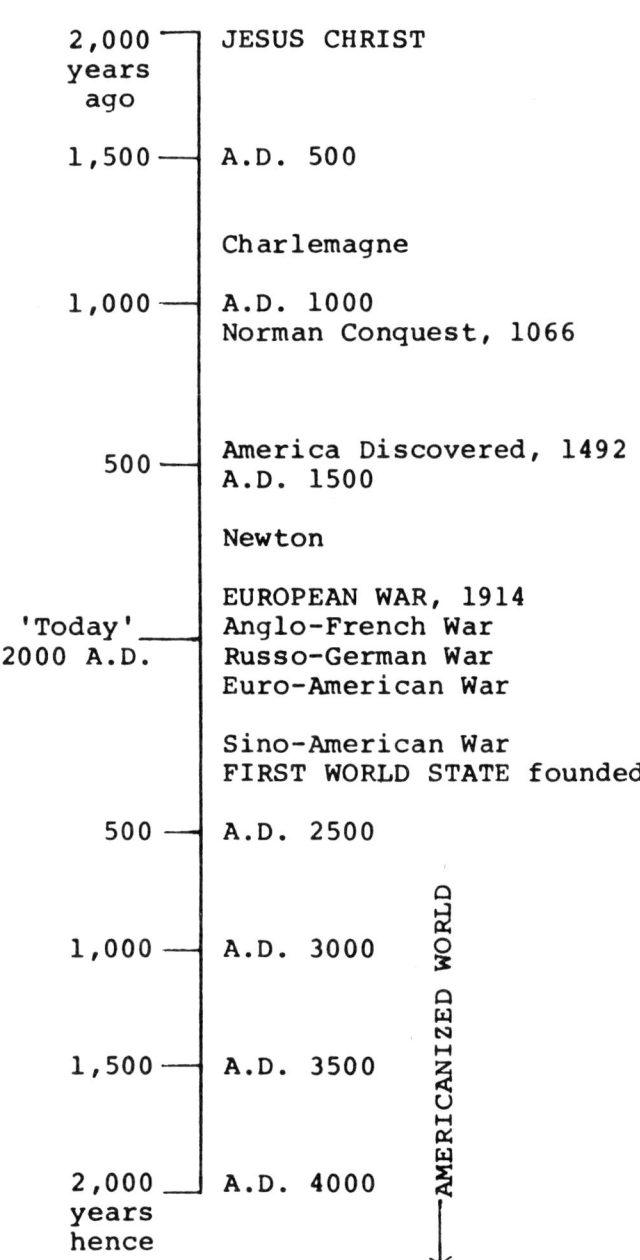

Long before a woman knows she's pregnant
And greets the news with fear or smiles
The news has head and heart and heart beats.
It's then no bigger than a tadpole.
The cells are working on that.
Although I never understood how
A radio set works, this cellular multiplicity
Comes within the realm of graspable ideas
And proves itself pure madness.
Those cells are programmed with the stuttering messages
Called life. Our generation's cracked
The code of life – we know about
The information in the genes inside the chromosomes.

Soon they'll have it all pegged,
Know which nucleic acid brings us curly hair
Which schizophrenic tendencies
Which gift of gab
Which stronger eyesight
Which sweet temper.
Because people are never content with being
Clever, they have to get cleverer.
They'll find the way, a century from now,
To make a synthetic gene, a splendid little thing,
To insert it – hypodermic gliding through the testicles –
Into the proto-embryo.

It'll be the end of us and the beginning
Of perfect people
Sweet temper artificially disseminated
a DNA utopia with never an angry word or
Cruel deed. Let's face it though
We hate change. The thought of perfection
Scares us the moment we
Have head and heart and heart beats.

You know why. Mischief's our common lot –
Original sin is not half as original
As perfection. Those better people

Would look back on us with a loving sorrow
As the Neanderthals of the pre-DNA Age.
In them the gaudy inferno of the undermind
Would droop and die and disappear
Unregretted – as with us, each generation
The Neanderthal dies from us
Our head and heart and heart beats.

This is the progression of the species
We can manage it for ourselves, thanks
From now on.

Future shock is a time phenomenon, a product of the greatly accelerated rate of change in society. It arises from the super-imposition of a new culture on an old one. It is culture shock in one's society. But its impact is far worse. For most Peace Corps men, in fact most travelers, have the comforting knowledge that the culture they left behind will be there to return to. The victim of future shock does not.

      Alvin Toffler : *Future Shock*

In our increasingly complex world, information is becoming the basic building block of society. However, at a time when the acquisition of new scientific information alone is approaching a rate of 250 million pages annually, the tide of knowledge is overwhelming the human capability for dealing with it. So man must turn to a machine if he hopes to contain the tide and channel it to beneficial ends.

      David Sarnoff : *No Life Untouched*

New technology disturbs the image, both private and corporate, in any society, so much so that fear and anxiety ensue and a new quest for identity has to begin. Nobody has ever studied what degree of innovation is required to shatter the self-image of a man or a society. In our time, at least, the amount of innovation far exceeds all the impacts of innovation of the past cultures of the world. We are more frantic to recover and put together the pieces of the shattered image than any past society whatever. It is this impulse that motivates the orgy of rear-view mirrorism, everything from the scholarly reconstruction of remote and dinky cultures to Gone With the Wind.

Marshall McLuhan : *War and Peace in the Global Village*

Ah, love, let us be true
To one another! for the world, which seems
To lie before us like a land of dreams,
So various, so beautiful, so new,
Hath really neither joy, nor love, nor light,
Nor certitude, nor peace, nor help for pain;
And we are here as on a darkling plain
Swept with confused alarms of struggle and flight,
Where ignorant armies clash by night.

    Matthew Arnold : *"Dover Beach"*

```
200,000 ──┐ Paleolithic Culture
years       'Heidelberg' Man
ago
            well established
150,000 ──

100,000 ── Eoanthropus

            ICE AGE (most recent)
            Mousterian Culture
50,000 ──   'Neanderthal' Man

            Late Paleolithic
            Neolithic
            Egyptian Pyramids
'Today'  ── Jesus Christ
2000 A.D.   FALL of the FIRST WORLD STATE

                    FIRST MEN
50,000 ──           IN
                    ECLIPSE

            Rise of PATAGONIA
100,000 ──  Fall of Patagonia

150,000 ──          FIRST MEN IN
                    ECLIPSE

200,000 ──
years               ↓
hence
```

MAN MAKES HIMSELF
(in memory of Friedrich Engels and Gordon Childe)

David Craig

The ape-man grips a clumsy axe
And ushers in the man.
But when he's cracked a bone with it
He lets it drop as done.

After five hundred thousand years
He chips the double edge
And stares at the advancing ice
Under his forehead ridge.

Soon he will think before he moves
And feel before he speaks
And cutting with the single edge
Discuss before he makes.

Soon he will eat the souls of bears,
Want what he cannot have,
And paint a bird he never saw
On the wall of a hidden cave.

Because of these two million years
The man is housed and shod
And upright (in the physical sense)
But still he dreams of gods.

Now he racks himself between
The body and the soul
And will not trust his mastery
Of language and of tool.

His eyes turn inwards more than out,
Look up and sigh for more,
And while his body rests, a soul
Creeps in at the back door.

How many generations more
Before our kingdom comes
And, dying and living for this world,
We make ourselves at home?

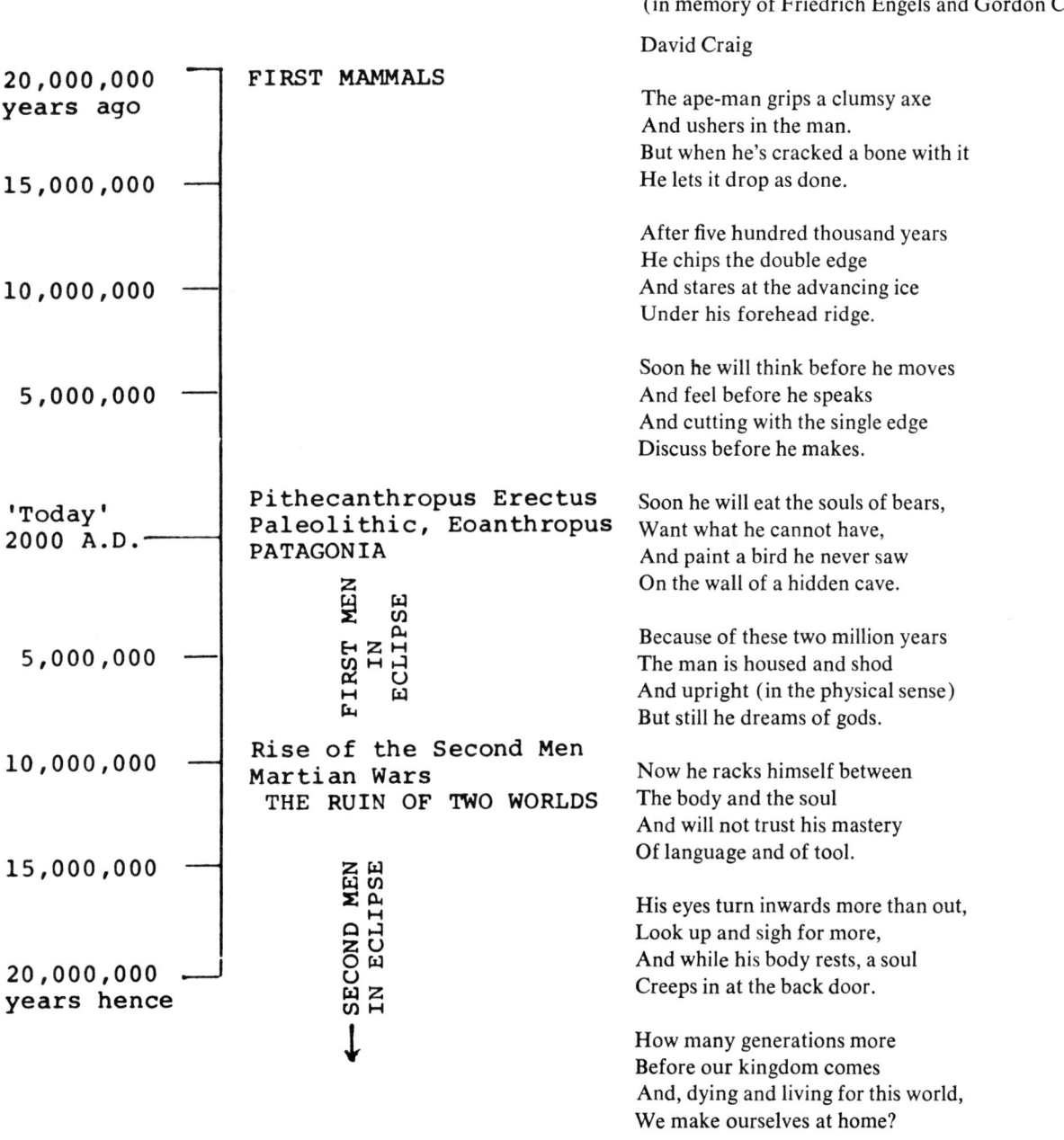

We are hurtling toward the time when we will be able to breed both super- and sub-races. As Theodore J. Gordon put it in *The Future*, "Given the ability to tailor the race, I wonder if we would 'create all men equal,' or would we choose to manufacture the DNA controllers; the humble servants; special athletes for the 'games'; research scientists with 200 IQ and diminutive bodies..." We shall have the power to produce races of morons or of mathematical savants.

       Alvin Toffler : *Future Shock*

The stars are in one's brain.

       Bertrand Russell

But innovation is more than a new method. It is a new view of the universe, as one of risk rather than of chance or of certainty. It is a new view of man's role in the universe; he creates order by taking risks. And this means that innovation, rather than being an assertion of human power, is an acceptance of human responsibility.

       Peter Drucker "*Landmarks of Tomorrow*"

Our period demands a type of man who can restore the lost equilibrium between inner and outer reality. This equilibrium, never static, but like reality itself, involved in continuous change, is like that of a tightrope dancer who, by small adjustments, keeps a continuous balance between his being and empty space. We need a type of man who can control his own existence by the process of balancing forces often regarded as irreconcilable; man is equipoise.

   Siegfried Giedion : "*Mechanization Takes Command*"

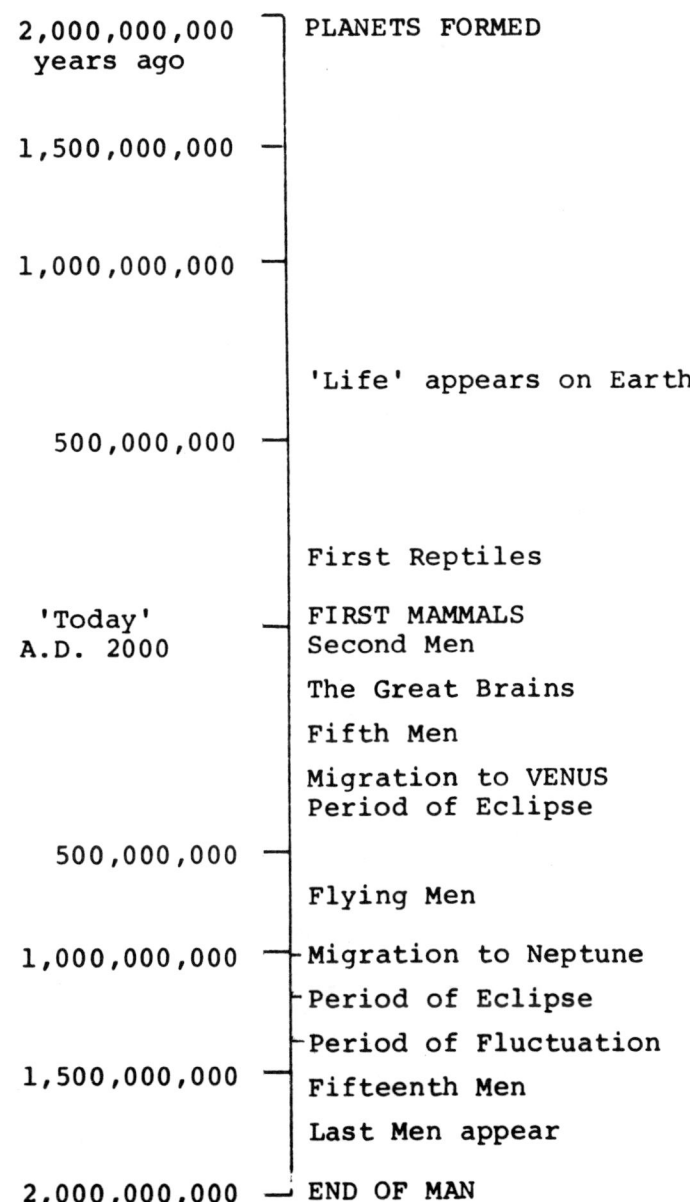

```
                    ⋮
          2 ──┼── First Stars formed
              ├── First Planets formed
              ├── Ichthyoid-Arachnoid Wars
              ├── Other Man begins,
          1       fluctuates,
              └── ends
10,000,000,000
    years  0 ──┼── Homo Sapiens begins, and
              │     attains industrialism
              └── Homo Sapiens ends on Neptune

              ── First Interstellar Travel
          1 ──
              ── First Artificial Planets
                    (as permanent abodes)

          2 ──┬── WAR OF WORLDS
              └── Symbiotics take charge

              ├── First Galactic Utopia
              ├── WAR OF STARS AND WORLDS
          3 ──
              ── SECOND GALACTIC UTOPIA

              ── First occurrence of Galactic
                                       Mind
          4 ──

              ├── First Colonization of Dead Stars
              ├── Partial Cosmical Utopia
              ├── First Occurrence of Cosmical Mind
              ├── Death of Last Surviving Star
          5 ──── SUPREME MOMENT OF THE COSMOS


          6 ──── DISSOLUTION OF THE COSMICAL MIND


              ── First Death of a Galaxy
          7 ──



          8 ──── Last Galaxy dies
```

LETTER TO A FUTURE GENERATION

Gwendolyn MacEwen

we did not anticipate you, you bright ones
though some of us saw you kneeling behind our bombs,
we did not fervently grow towards you
for most of us grew backwards
sowing our seed in the black fields of history

avoid monuments, engrave our names beneath your own
for you have consumed our ashes by now
for you have one quiet mighty language by now

do not excavate our cities
to catalogue the objects of our doom
but burn all you find to make yourselves room,
you have no need of archaeology,
your faces are your total history

for us it was necessary to invent a darkness,
to subtract light in order to see,
for us it was certain death to know our names
as they were written in the black books of history

I stand with an animal at my left hand
and a warm, breathing ghost at my right
saying, Remember that this letter was made
for you to burn, that its meaning lies
only in your burning it,
that its lines await your cleansing fire –
understand it only insofar
as that warm ghost at my right hand breathed
down my blood and for a moment wrote the lines
while guns sounded out from a mythical city
and destroyed the times

CUPID'S GRIN
For Sterling Bunnell

Michael McClure

      YES! THIS DAMN UNIVERSE!
   An ever-flowing, eternal, closed up,
  open system – a dial of vibratory flows
from end to front – a technicolor timeless object –
   STARS – STARS – NEBULAE – AND SWIRLS
   of growing energy that fantasizes self.
     A LIVING STATUE OF A SONG!
     (Amoeba daydreams Metazoa.
     Helium imagines Milky Way!
     Or start from either end.)
       ALIVE AS THE SEA!
       When it all begins
        I'll be there.
    You'll know me by my curling lips
       – AND CHUCKLE
          !

Today, nowhere in the world are there elders who know what the children know, no matter how remote and simple the societies are in which the children live. In the past there were always some elders who knew more than any children in terms of their experience of having grown up within a cultural system. Today there are none. It is not only that parents are no longer guides, but that there are no guides, whether one seeks them in one's own country or abroad. There are no elders who know what those who have been reared within the last twenty years know about the world into which they were born.

We must place the future, like the unborn child in the womb of a woman, within a community of men, women, and children, among us, already here, already to be nourished and succored and protected, already in need of things for which, if they are not prepared before it is born, it will be too late. So, as the young say, The Future Is Now.

Margaret Mead : *Culture and Commitment*

The face of change is a young one – and it comes in many colors. All previous revolutions had, as their goal, the attainment of some new state of equilibrium. What we are seeing in our time is a new order of revolution, whose goal is not a new equilibrium, but social disorder itself. It is the first social recognition that continuous change itself is a form of equilibrium – and that it is only in disorder that we find order. These kids are "surfing" and it is the essence of surfing that one should ride the turbulence without succumbing to it. You cannot have fun surfing on a slow wave – and you cannot surf at all on a frozen one.

Don Fabun : *The Dynamics of Change*

The most important part about tomorrow is not the technology or the automation, but that man is going to come into entirely new relationships with his fellow men. He will retain much more in his everyday life of what we term the naïveté and idealism of the child. I think the way to see what tomorrow is going to look like is just to look at our children.

R. Buckminster Fuller

THE CITY OF THE END OF THINGS

Archibald Lampman

Beside the pounding cataracts
Of midnight streams unknown to us
'Tis builded in the leaflets tracts
And valleys huge of Tartarus.
Lurid and lofty and vast it seems;
It hath no rounded name that rings,
But I have heard it called in dreams
The City of the End of Things.

Its roofs and iron towers have grown
None knoweth how high within the night,
But in its murky streets far down
A flaming terrible and bright
Shakes all the stalking shadows there,
Across the walls, across the floors,
And shifts upon the upper air
From out a thousand furnace doors;
And all the while an awful sound
Keeps roaring on continually,
And crashes in the ceaseless round
Of a gigantic harmony.
Through its grim depths re-echoing
And all its weary height of walls,
With measured roar and iron ring,
The inhuman music lifts and falls.
Where no thing rests and no man is,
And only fire and night hold sway;
The beat, the thunder, and the hiss
Cease not, and change not, night nor day.
And moving at unheard commands,
The abysses and vast fires between,
Flit figures that with clanking hands
Obey a hideous routine;
They are not flesh, they are not bone,
They see not with the human eye,
And from their iron lips is blown
A dreadful and monotonous cry;
And whose of our mortal race
Should find that city unaware,
Lean Death would smite him face to face,
And blanch him with its venomed air:
Or caught by the terrific spell,
Each thread of memory snapt and cut,
His soul would shrivel and its shell
Go rattling like an empty nut.

It was not always so, but once,
In days that no man thinks upon,
Fair voices echoed from its stones,
The light above it leaped and shone:
Once there were multitudes of men,
That built that city in their pride,
Until its might was made, and then
They withered age by age and died.
But now of that prodigious race,
Three only in an iron tower,
Set like carved idols face to face,
Remain the masters of its power;
And at the city gate a fourth,
Gigantic and with dreadful eyes,
Sits looking toward the lightless north,
Beyond the reach of memories;
Fast rooted to the lurid floor,
A bulk that never moves a jot,
In his pale body dwells no more,
Or mind or soul, – an idiot!
But sometime in the end those three
Shall perish and their hands be still.
And with the master's touch shall flee
Their incommunicable skill.
A stillness absolute as death
Along the slacking wheels shall lie,
And, flagging at a single breath,
The fires shall moulder out and die.
The roar shall vanish at its height,
And over that tremendous town
The silence of eternal night
Shall gather close and settle down.
All its grim grandeur, tower and hall,
Shall be abandoned utterly,
And into rust and dust shall fall
From century to century;
Nor ever living thing shall grow,
Nor trunk of tree, nor blade of grass;
No drop shall fall, no wind shall blow,
Nor sound of any foot shall pass:
Alone of its accursed state,
One thing the hand of Time shall spare,
For the grim Idiot at the gate
Is deathless and eternal there.

elegy for three astronauts

```
        w  w  w

        i  i  i

        d  d  d

a s t r           n a u t

a s t r     O     n a u t

a s t r           n a u t

        w  w  w

        i  i  i

        d  d  d

        o  o  o

        w  w  w
```

A HELL OF A DAY

Tim Reynolds

This was a day of fumbling and petty accidents,
as though the population had grown all thumbs
at once. Watering her chrysanthemums,
Mrs. Kamei was surprised to see the plants
blacken, water turn to steam. Both Dote
and Michilo noted the other's absence but
not her own.
Mr. Kime lifted his hat, but his head was gone.
Mr. Watanable rolled a double zero.
Photographing her son by the river bridge
Mrs. Ume pressed the shutter and overexposed
her film.
Her son's yawn swallowed him. And everything
turned on when pretty Miss Mihara snapped the
light switch
Then old Mr. Ekahomo struck a match
to light his pipe, and the town caught, and
dissolved in flame.

I HAVE SEEN THE ROBINS FALL

Louis Dudek

I have seen the robins fall
One by one, from the trees, their throats dry;
And I have heard their music cease,
Stalked to silence in the high stark trees.

The fingers of grass I have seen bent
In the dry air, and split to sharp forks;
The sea dashing on a dandelion
Crusted, and turned to rusted iron.

I have seen a white salt spread on your stones,
With the crushed powder of pure, white bones,
And all the poems that sang in my heart
Turned to the same white, bitter salt.

EARTH

John Hall Wheelock

"A planet doesn't explode of itself," said drily
The Martian astronomer, gazing off into the air –
"That they were able to do it is proof that highly
Intelligent beings must have been living there."

Then I saw a new heaven and a new earth for the first heaven and the first earth had passed away, and the sea was no more. And I saw the holy city, new Jerusalem, coming down out of heaven from God, prepared as a bride adorned for her husband; and I heard a great voice from the throne saying, "Behold, the dwelling of God is with men. He will dwell with them, and they shall be his people," and God himself will be with them; he will wipe away every tear from their eyes, and death shall be no more, neither shall there be mourning nor crying nor pain any more, for the former things have passed away."

And he who sat upon the throne said, "Behold, I make all things new." Also he said, "Write this, for these words are trustworthy and true." And he said to me, "it is done! I am the Alpha and the Omega, the beginning and the end. To the thirsty I will give water without price from the fountain of the water of life. He who conquers shall have this heritage, and I will be his God and he shall be my son. But as for the cowardly, the faithless, the polluted, as for murderers, fornicators, sorcerers, idolaters, and all liars, their lot shall be in the lake that burns with fire and brimstone, which is the second death."

Revelation 21: 1-8

```
                                    astronaut
                                    satronau
                                    starona
                                    staron
                                    staro
                                    star
                                     stars
                                      starsa
                                       starsai
                                        starsail
                                         starsailo
                                          starsailor
            starsailor
            satrsailo
            astrsao
            astrso
          astro
           astron
            astrona
             astronau
              astronaut
                                    astronaut
                                    satronau
                                    starona
                                    staron
                                    staro
                                    star
                                     stars
                                      starsa
                                       starsai
                                        starsail
                                         starsailo
                                          starsailor
```

D.O.M., A.D. 2167

John Frederick Nims

When I've outlived three plastic
   hearts, or four,
Another's kidneys, corneas (*beep!*)
   with more
Unmentionable rubber, nylon, such –
And when (*beep!*) in a steel drawer
   (DO NOT TOUCH!),
Mere brain cells in a saline wash, I
   thrive
With thousands, taped to quaver out,
   "Alive!" –
God grant that steel two wee (*beep!*)
   eyes of glass
To glitter wicked when the nurses pass.

EARTH

Oliver Herford

If this little world tonight
   Suddenly should fall through space
In a hissing, headlong flight,
   Shrivelling from off its face,
As it falls into the sun,
   In an instant every trace
Of the little crawling things –
   Ants, philosophers, and lice,
Cattle, cockroaches, and kings,
   Beggars, millionaires, and mice,
Men and maggots all as one
As it falls into the sun . . .
Who can say but at the same
   Instant from some planet far
A child may watch us and exclaim:
   "See the pretty shooting star!"

A.D. 2267

John Frederick Nims

Once on the gritty moon (burnt earth hung far
In the black, rhinestone sky – lopsided star),
Two gadgets, with great fishbowls for a head,
Feet clubbed, hips loaded, shoulders bent. She said,
"Fantasies haunt me. A green garden. Two
Lovers aglow in flesh. The pools so blue!"
He whirrs with masculine pity, "Can't forget
Old superstitions? The earth-legend yet?"

In the past, men could shrug their shoulders in the face of most of the evils of life because they were powerless to prevent them. . . . Now there is no one to blame but ourselves. Nothing is any longer inevitable. Since everything can be accomplished, everything must be deliberately chosen. It is in human power for the first time to achieve a level of human welfare exceeding our wildest imaginings or to commit race suicide, slowly or rapidly. The choice rests only with us.

           Jerome D. Frank : "*Galloping Technology: A New Social Disease*"

* MAN * IN * ORBIT *
*   *   *   *

D. O. Pitches

```
        ******
    *While*freighting*f
  rom*Earth*to*Venus*we
  *passed*a*man*without*a*
 spacesuit.*He*was*not*pleasant
  *to*look*at,*orbiting*the*Sun.
   *And*I*remembered*how*he*w
   ould*repeat*a*modish*phrase*ba
   ck*on*Earth,*endlessly — *Stop*
       the*world,*I*want*to*get
        *off.*And*it*appeared*t
           hat**someone*had.*
             ******
```

MAN seems to be entering one of the major crises of his career. His whole future, nay the possibility of his having any future at all, depends on the turn which events may take in the next half-century. It is a commonplace that he is coming into possession of new and dangerous instruments for controlling his environment and his own nature. Perhaps it is less obvious that he is also groping toward a new view of his office in the scheme of things, and toward a new and racial purpose. Unfortunately he may possibly take too long to learn what it is that he really wants to do with himself. Before he can gain clear insight, he may lose himself in a vast desert of spiritual aridity, or even blunder into physical self-destruction. Nothing can save him but a new vision, and a consequent new order of sanity, or common sense.

           Olaf Stapledon : *Last and First Men*

THE TRUANT

E. J. Pratt

"What have you there?" the great Panjandrum said
To the Master of the Revels who had led
A bucking truant with a stiff backbone
Close to the foot of the Almighty's throne.

"Right Reverend, most adored,
And forcibly acknowledged Lord
By the keen logic of your two-edged sword!

This creature has presumed to classify
Himself – a biped, rational, six feet high
And two feet wide; weights fourteen stone;
Is guilty of a multitude of sins.
He has abjured his choric origins,
And like an undomesticated slattern,
Walks with tangential step unknown
Within the weave of the atomic pattern.
He has developed concepts, grins
Obscenely at your Royal bulletins,
Possesses what he calls a will
Which challenges your power to kill."

"What is his pedigree?"

"The base is guaranteed, your Majesty –
Calcium, carbon, phosphorus, vapour
And other fundamentals spun
From the umbilicus of the sun,
And yet he says he will not caper
Around your throne, nor toe the rules
For the ballet of the fiery molecules."

"His concepts and denials – scrap them, burn them –
To the chemists with them promptly."

                             "Sire,
The stuff is not amenable to fire.
Nothing but their own kind can overturn them.
The chemists have sent back the same old story –
"With our extreme gelatinous apology,
We beg to inform your Imperial Majesty,
Unto who be dominion and power and glory,
There still remains that strange precipitate
Which has the quality to resist
Our oldest and most trusted catalyst,
It is a substance we cannot cremate
By temperatures known to our Laboratory.' "

And the great Panjandrum's face grew dark –
"I'll put those chemists to their annual purge
And I myself shall be the thaumaturge
To find the nature of this fellow's spark.
Come, bring him nearer by yon halter rope:
I'll analyse him with the cosmoscope."

Pulled forward; with his neck awry,
The little fellow six feet short,
Aware he was about to die,
Committed grave contempt of court
By answering with a flinchless stare

The ALL HIGH swore until his face was black.
He called him a coprophagite,
A genus *homo,* egomaniac,
Third cousin to the family of worms.
A sporozoan from the ooze of night,
Spawn of a spavined troglodyte:
He swore by all the catalogue of terms
Known since the slang of carboniferous Time.
He said that he could trace him back
To pollywogs and earwigs in the slime.
And in his shrillest tenor he began
Reciting his indictment of the man,
Until he closed upon this capital crime –
"You are accused of singing out of key
(A foul unmitigated dissonance),
Of shuffling in the measures of the dance,
Then walking out with that defiant, free
Toss of your head, banging the doors,
Leaving a stench upon the jacinth floors.
You have fallen like a curse
On the mechanics of my Universe.

"Herewith I measure out your penalty –
Hearken while you hear, look while you see;
I send you now upon your homeward route
Where you shall find
Humiliation for your pride of mind.
I shall make deaf the ear, and dim the eye,
Put palsy in your touch, make mute
Your speech, intoxicate your cells and dry
Your blood and marrow, shoot
Arthritic needles through your cartilage,
And having parched you with old age,
I'll pass you wormwise through the mire;
And when your rebel will
Is mouldered, all desire
Shrivelled, all your concepts broken,
Backward in dust I'll blow you till

You join my spiral festival of fire.
Go, Masters of the Revels – I have spoken."

And the little genus *homo,* six feet high,
Standing erect, countered with this reply –
"You dumb insouciant invertebrate,
You rule a lower than a feudal state –
A realm of flunkey decimals that run,
Return: return and run; again return,
Each group around its little sun,
And every sun a satellite.
There they go by day and night,
Nothing to do but run and burn,
Taking turn and turn about,
Light-year in and light-year out,
Dancing, dancing in quadrillions,
Never leaving their pavilions.

"Your astronomical conceit
Of bulk and power is anserine.
Your ignorance so thick,
You did not know your own arithmetic.
We flung the graphs about your flying feet;
We measured your diameter –
Merely a line
Of zeros prefaced by an integer.
Before we came
You had no name.
You did not know direction or your pace;
We taught you all you ever knew
Of motion, time, and space.
We healed you of your vertigo
And put you in our kindergarten show,
Perambulated you through prisms, drew
Your mileage through the Milky Way,
Lassoed your comets when they ran astray,
Yoked Leo, Taurus, and your team of Bears
To pull our kiddy cars of inverse squares.

"Boast not about your harmony,
Your perfect curves, your rings
Of *pure and endless light* – 'Twas we
Who pinned upon your Seraphim their wings,
And when your brassy heavens rang
With joy that morning while the planets sang
Their choruses of archangelic lore,
'Twas we who ordered the notes upon their score
Out of our winds and strings.
Yes! all our shapley forms
Are ours – parabolas of silver light,
Those blueprints of your spiral stairs
From nadir depth of zenith height,
Coronas, rainbows after storms,
Auroras on your eastern tapestries
And constellations over western seas.

"And when, one day, grown conscious of your age,
While pondering an eolith,
We turned a human page
And blotted out a cosmic myth
With all its baby symbols to explain
The sunlight in Apollo's eyes,
Our rising pulses and the birth of pain,
Fear, and that fern-and-fungus breath
Stalking our nostrils to our caves of death –
That day we learned how to anatomize
Your body, calibrate your size
And set a mirror up before your face
To show you what you really were – a rain
Of dull Lucretian atoms crowding space,
A series of concentric waves which any fool
Might make by dropping stones within a pool,
Or an exploding bomb forever in flight
Bursting like hell through Chaos and Old Night.

"You oldest of the hierarchs
Composed of electronic sparks,
We grant you speed,
We grant you power, and fire
That ends in ash, but we concede
To you no pain nor joy nor love nor hate,
No final tableau of desire,
No causes won or lost, no free
Adventure at the outposts – only
The degradation of your energy
When at some late
Slow number of your dance your sergeant –
  major Fate
Will catch you blind and groping and will send
You reeling on that long and lonely
Lockstep of your wave-lengths towards you end.

"We who have met
With stubborn calm the dawn's hot fusillades;
Who have seen the forehead sweat
Under the tug of pulleys on the joints,
Under the liquidating tally
Of the cat-and-truncheon bastinades;
Who have taught our souls to rally
To mountain horns and the sea's rockets
When the needle ran demented through the points;
We who have learned to clench
Our fists and raise our lightless sockets
To morning skies after the midnight raids,
Yet cocked our ears to bugles on the barricades
And in cathedral rubble found a way to quench
A dying thirst within a Galilean valley –
No! by the Rood, we will not join your ballet."

END OF THE SEERS' CONVENTION

Kenneth Fearing

We were walking and talking on the roof of the world,
In an age that seemed, at that time, an extremely modern age
Considering a merger, last on the agenda, of the Seven Great
    Leagues that held the Seven True Keys of the Seven
    Ultimate Spheres of all moral, financial, and occult life.

"I foresee a day," said one of the delegates, an astroanalyst from
    Idaho, "when men will fly through the air, and talk across space
They will sail in ships that float beneath the water;
They will emanate shadows of themselves upon a screen, and the
    shadows will move, and talk, and seem as though real."

"Very interesting, indeed," declared a Gypsy delegate. "But I should
    like to ask, as a simple reader of tea leaves and palms;
How does this combat the widespread and growing evil of the police?"
The astrologer shrugged, and an accidental meteor fell from his robes
    and smoldered on the floor.
"In addition," he said, "I foresee a war,
And a victory after that one, and after the victory, a war again."

"Trite," was the comment of a crystal-gazer from Miami Beach.
"Any damnfool, at any damn time, can visualize wars, and more wars,
    and famines and plagues.
The real question is: How to seize power from entrenched and
    organized men of Common Sense?"

"I foresee a day," said the Idaho astrologer, "when human beings will
    live on top of flag-poles,
And dance, at some profit, for weeks and months without any rest,
And some will die very happily of eating watermelons, and nails, and
    cherry pies."

"Why," said a bored numerologist, reaching for his hat, "can't these
    star-gazers keep their feet on the ground?"
"Even if it's true," said a Bombay illusionist, "it is not, like the
    rope-trick, altogether practical."
"And furthermore, and finally," shouted the astrologer, with comets and
    halfmoons dropping from his pockets, and his agitated sleeves,

"I prophesy an age of triumph for laziness and sleep, and dreams and
    utter peace.
I can see couples walking through the public parks in love, and those
    who do not are wanted by the sheriff.
I see men fishing beside quiet streams, and those who do not are
    pursued by collectors, and plastered with liens."

"This does not tell us how to fight against skepticism," muttered a
    puzzled mesmerist, groping for the door.
"I think" agreed a lady who interpreted the cards, "we are all inclined
    to accept too much on faith."
A sprinkling of rain, or dragon's blood,
Or a handful of cinders fell on the small, black umbrellas they raised
    against the sky.

This world of ours is a new world, in which the unity of knowledge, the nature of human communities, the order of society, the order of ideas, the very notions of society and culture have changed, and will not return to what they have been in the past.

What is new is new not because it has never been there before, but because it has changed in quality . . .

One thing that is new is the prevalence of newness, the changing scale and scope of change itself, so that the world alters as we walk in it, so that the years of a man's life measure not some small growth or rearrangement or moderation of what he learned in childhood, but a great upheaval.

Robert Oppenheimer

The world of today . . . is as different from the world in which I was born as that world was from Julius Caesar's. I was born in the middle of human history, to date, roughly. Almost as much has happened since I was born as happened before.

Alvin Toffler : *Future Shock*

For the existence of any science, it is necessary that there exist phenomena which do not stand isolated. In a world ruled by a succession of miracles performed by an irrational God subject to sudden whims, we should be forced to await each new catastrophe in a state of perplexed passiveness.

We have a picture of such a world in the croquet game in *Alice in Wonderland*: where the mallets are flamingoes; the balls, hedgehogs, which quietly unroll and go about their own business; the hoops, playing-card soldiers, likewise subject to locomotor initiative of their own; and the rules are decrees of the testy, unpredictable Queen of Hearts.

Norbert Wiener : "*Cybernetics*"

Even the most troubled epoch is worthy of respect, because it is the work not just of a few people but of humanity; and thus it is the work of creative nature — which is often cruel but never absurd. If this epoch in which we are living is a cruel one it is more than our duty to love it, to penetrate it with our love till we have removed the heavy weight of matter screening the light that shines on the farther side.

Pauwels and Bergier : *The Morning of the Magicians*

SPACE HYMN

Lothar and the Hand People

Standing on the moon
Filled with thoughts of home
Earth so slowly turning

Twenty thousand years
Human hopes and fears
Are we finally learning

Riders together on a starship of stone
Living together, dreaming together
Dying alone

WHAT I EXPECTED

Stephen Spender

What I expected was
Thunder, fighting,
Long struggles with men
And climbing.
After continual straining
I should grow strong;
Then the rocks would shake
And I should rest long.

What I had not foreseen
Was the gradual day
Weakening the will
Leaking the brightness away,
The lack of good to touch
The fading of body and soul
Like smoke before wind
Corrupt, unsubstantial.

The wearing of Time,
And the watching of cripples pass
With limbs shaped like questions
In their odd twist,
The pulverous grief
Melting the bones with pity,
The sick falling from earth —
These, I could not foresee.

For I had expected always
Some brightness to hold in trust,
Some final innocence
To save from dust;
That, hanging solid,
Would dangle through all
Like the created poem
Or the dazzling crystal.

Prophets, in the modern sense of the word, have never existed. Jonah was no prophet in the modern sense, for his prophecy of Nineveh failed. Every honest man is a Prophet; he utters his opinion both of private and public matters. Thus: if you go on So, the result is So. He never says, such a thing shall happen let you do what you will. A Prophet is a Seer, not an Arbitrary Dictator. It is man's fault if God is not able to do him good, for he gives to the just and to the unjust, but the unjust reject his gift.

    William Blake : *Selected Poetry and Prose of Blake*

Lead, kindly fowl! They always did: ask the ages. What bird has done yesterday man may do next year, be it fly, be it moult, be it hatch, be it agreement in the nest.

    James Joyce : *Finnegans Wake*

To tell you that we must all work and struggle and revolt against those who live in yesterday, before all our tomorrows are stolen away from us

    Harlan Ellison : *The Glass Teat*

Behind every man now alive stand thirty ghosts, for that is the ratio by which the dead outnumber the living. Since the dawn of time, roughly a hundred billion human beings have walked the planet Earth.

Now this is an interesting number, for by a curious coincidence there are approximately a hundred billion stars in our local universe, the Milky Way. So for every man who has ever lived, in this universe there shines a star.

But every one of those stars is a sun, often far more brilliant and glorious than the small, nearby star we call the Sun. And many – perhaps most – of those alien suns have planets circling them. So almost certainly there is enough land in the sky to give every member of the human species, back to the first apeman, his own private, world-sized heaven – or hell.

How many of those potential heavens and hells are now inhabited, and by what manner of creatures, we have no way of guessing; the very nearest is a million times farther away than Mars or Venus, those still remote goals of the next generation. But the barriers of distance are crumbling; one day we shall meet our equals, or our masters, among the stars.

    Arthur C. Clarke : *2001: A Space Odyssey*

I SAW A MAN WITH POPPIES

Michael Johnson

I saw a man with poppies
in his hair,
whose bones shone through

his clothes, hold up
an hourglass
in his skinless hand.

He watched the grain of silver
fill the glass; then took
the wreath of poppies

from his head
and gave it to me.
The hourglass cracked,

I saw
his bones white-hot
my hands

a crimson red,
and ditches filled
with fly-brown

horses,
mud
and men.

THE SECOND COMING

W. B. Yeats

Turning and turning in the widening gyre
The falcon cannot hear the falconer;
Things fall apart; the centre cannot hold;
Mere anarchy is loosed upon the world,
The blood-dimmed tide is loosed, and everywhere
The ceremony of innocence is drowned;
The best lack all conviction, while the worst
Are full of passionate intensity.

Surely some revelation is at hand;
Surely the Second Coming is at hand.
The Second Coming!   Hardly are those words out
When a vast image out of *Spiritus Mundi*
Troubles my sight: somewhere in sands of the desert
A shape with lion body and the head of a man,
A gaze blank and pitiless as the sun,
Is moving its slow thighs, while all about it
Reel shadows of the indignant desert birds.
The darkness drops again; but now I know
That twenty centuries of stony sleep
Were vexed to nightmare by a rocking cradle,
And what rough beast, its hour come round at last,
Slouches towards Bethlehem to be born?

I believe we can create a better society. I believe that man can abolish toil and abolish it well before the end of this century, that he can develop, instead, work. I see man working in four areas: first, self-development – both mental and physical; second, the human care of human beings; third, the whole area of human relationships. It takes a lifetime to get to know somebody, and if you don't like to call it "work," I don't care. It's still something to do, and that's what worries a lot of people: What will man do next? Fourth, politics – the creation of a good community.

    Robert Theobald : *Dialogue on Poverty*

The past is but the beginning of the beginning, and all that is and has been is but the twilight of the dawn. A day will come when beings who are now latent in our thoughts and hidden in our loins . . . shall laugh and reach out their hands amid the stars.

    H. G. Wells : *The Discovery of the Future*

A BITTER MORNING

J. W. Hackett

A bitter morning:
Sparrows sitting together
Without any necks.

Now I a fourfold vision see,
And a fourfold vision is given to me;
'Tis fourfold in soft Beulah's night
And twofold Always. May God us keep
From Single vision and Newton's sleep

    William Blake : *Letter to Butts*

There lies before us, if we choose, continual progress in happiness, knowledge, and wisdom. Shall we, instead, choose death, because we cannot forget our quarrels? We appeal, as human beings to human beings. Remember your humanity, and forget the rest. If you can do so, the way lies open to a new Paradise; if you cannot, there lies before you the risk of universal death.

The Russell-Einstein Appeal, July 9, 1955

ACKNOWLEDGEMENTS

This page constitutes an extension of the copyright page. We gratefully acknowledge the assistance of the copyright holders in granting permission to reprint the following copyrighted materials. Every effort has been made to locate the copyright holder; any errors or omissions drawn to our attention will be corrected in future editions.

"Nimble Rays of Day Bring Oxygen to her Blood", from Tom Clark, *Stones*, copyright © 1969 by Tom Clark, all rights reserved. Reprinted by permission of Harper & Rown, Inc.

"An Old Man's Winter Night", "Out, Out . . .", from *The Poetry of Robert Frost*, edited by Edward Connery Lathem. Copyright 1916, © 1969 by Holt, Rinehart and Winston, Inc. Copyright 1944 by Robert Frost. Reprinted by permission of Holt, Rinehart and Winston, Inc., New York.

"The Game" by permission of F. R. Scott.
"Because Growing a Mustache Was Pretty Tiring", from Kenneth Patchen, *Because it is*. Copyright © 1960 by New Directions Publishing Corp. Reprinted by permission of New Directions Publishing Corp.
"It's Outside", "Fountain", "But Even So", "Can't Recall Me One Reason", "Loving", from Kenneth Patchen, But Even So. Copyright © 1968 by Kenneth Patchen. Reprinted by permission of New Directions Publishing Corp.

"A Little Child", "The World Upside Down", "Butterflies", "The Frost", from Harold G. Henderson, *Introduction to Haiku*, copyright © 1958 by Harold G. Henderson. Reprinted by permission of Doubleday & Company, Inc.
"Warty Bliggens the Toad", from Don Marquis, *The Lives and Times of archie and mehitabel*, copyright 1927 by Doubleday & Company, Inc.
"Innocence", from Thom Gunn, *My Sad Captains*, by permission of Faber and Faber Ltd and University of Chicago Press.

"The Reason for Skylarks", "The Origin of Baseball", "Avarice and Ambition", "Gautama in the Deer Park in Benares", "The Orange Bears", "Have You Killed Your Man For To-Day?", "How to be an Army", "Let Us Have Madness", "Fall of the Evening Star", "We Leave You Pleasure", from Kenneth Patchen, *Collected Poems*. Copyright 1936, 1943 by Kenneth Patchen, copyright 1939, 1942, 1949 by New Directions Publishing Corp. Reprinted by permission of New Directions Publishing Corp.

"In It", from George Johnston, *The Cruising Auk*, "The Sorcerer", from A. J. M. Smith, *Collected Poems*, and "They Arose" by Paul Hiebert, reprinted by permission of the Oxford University Press, Canadian Branch.
"On Being Asked for a War Poem", "The Second Coming", "Crazy Janes Talks With the Bishop", from W. B. Yeats, *Collected Poems*, by permission of Michael Butler Yeats, Macmillan Ltd., London, and The Macmillan Company of Canada Limited.

"Protocols", "The Death of the Ball Turret Gunner", copyright © by Mrs. Randall Jarrell, from Randall Jarrell, *The Complete Poems*, by permission of Farrar, Straus and Giroux, Inc.
"Chansons Innocents", "Buffalo Bill's Defunct", "pity this busy monster, manunkind", by e. e. cummings, by permission of Harcourt, Brace, Jovanovich, Inc.
"Circles in the Sand", "Worms and the Wind", "Explanations of Love", and "Mag", by Carl Sandburg, by permission of Harcourt, Brace, Jovanovich, Inc.

"Au Jardin des Plantes", from John Wain, *Weep Before God*, by permission of Macmillan Ltd., London, and The Macmillan Company of Canada Limited.
"I Wanted to Smash", "Evening in the Suburbs", from Raymond Souster, *The Colour of the Times*, by permission of The Ryerson Press, McGraw-Hill of Canada Limited.
"Heirloom", from A. M. Klein, *Hath Not A Jew*, published by Behrman House Inc., reprinted by permission of The Ryerson Press, McGraw-Hill of Canada Limited.

"Letter to a Future Generation", "You Held Out The Light", "Fire Gardens", from Gwendolyn MacEwen, *The Shadow Maker*, published by The Macmillan Company of Canada
"The Truant", from E. J. Pratt, *Collected Poems*, published by The Macmillan Company of Canada Ltd.
"The Taxi", from Amy Lowell, *Complete Poetical Works of Amy Lowell*, by permission of Houghton Mifflin Company.

"The Seafarer", "Ancient Music", from Ezra Pound, *Personae*. Copyright 1926 by Ezra Pound. Reprinted by permission of New Directions Publishing Corp.
"Thursday", "Young Woman at a Window", "To a Poor Old Woman", from William Carlos Williams, *Collected Earlier Poems*. Copyright 1938 by William Carlos Williams. Reprinted by permission of New Directions Publishing Corp.
"Ride A Wild Horse" by Hannah Kahn. First published as "Into the Sun" in *Saturday Review*, March 21, 1953. Copyright 1953 The Saturday Review Associates, Inc.

"Indian Reservation: Caughnawaga", from A. M. Klein, *The Rocking Chair*, by permission of The Ryerson Press, McGraw-Hill Company of Canada Limited.
"Fortune has its cookies . . .", "Christ climbed down", "Dog", from Lawrence Ferlinghetti, *A Coney Island of the Mind*. Copyright 1955, © 1958 by Lawrence Ferlinghetti. Reprinted by permission of New Directions Publishing Corp.
"Elephants", from John Newlove, *Elephants, Mothers & Others*, by permission of the author.

"Take One Home For The Kiddies", from Philip Larkin, *The Whitsun Weddings*, copyright © 1960 by Philip Larkin, by permission of Faber and Faber Ltd and Random House, Inc., Alfred A. Knopf, Inc.
"The Horses", from Edwin Muir, *Collected Poems 1921-1958*, copyright © 1960 by Willa Muir, reprinted by permission of Faber and Faber Ltd and Oxford University Press.
"Say This City Has Ten Million Souls", from W. H. Auden, *Collected Shorter Poems 1927-1957*, reprinted by permission of Faber and Faber Ltd and Alfred A. Knopf, Inc.

"Traveling Through the Dark", from William Stafford, *Traveling Through the Dark*, copyright © 1960 by William Stafford, reprinted by permission of Harper & Row, Publishers, Inc.
"The Man in the Dead Machine", from Donald Hall, *The Alligator Bride*, copyright © 1969 by Donald Hall, copyright © 1966 The New Yorker Magazine, Inc. Reprinted by permission of Harper & Row, Inc.
"Schoolchildren", from W. H. Auden, *Collected Shorter Poems 1927-1957*, by permission of Faber and Faber Ltd.

"Earth", from Oliver Herford, *The Bashful Earthquake*, by permission of Charles Scribner's Sons.
"Little Johnny's Confession", from Brian Patten, *Little Johnny's Confession*, published by George Allen and Unwin Ltd.
"Stupid", from Graham Thomas, *It's World That Makes The Love Go Round* (Corgi Books). First published in *Second Aeon* (Cardiff). Reprinted by permission of the author.
"Thug", by Raymond Garlick, by permission of the author.
"Demolition" by Norman Iles, by permission of the author.

"A Prayer", from *Postwar Polish Poetry*, ed. Czeslaw Nilosz, copyright © 1965 by Czeslaw Nilosz. Reprinted by permission of Doubleday & Company, Inc.
"One Who Hopes", "The Little Man With Wooden Hair", from Kenneth Patchen, *Hurrah for Anything*. Copyright © 1957 by New Directions Publishing Corp. Reprinted by permission of New Directions Publishing Corp.
"Hunger", by Ulli Beier, from *Poems of Black Africa*, ed. Langston Hughes, copyright © by Langston Hughes. Reprinted by permission of Indiana University Press.

"How They Made The Golem", "Riverdale Lion", "Passion", from John Robert Colombo, *Abracadabra*, reprinted by permission of The Canadian Publishers, McClelland and Stewart Limited.
"Six Young Men", from Ted Hughes, *The Hawk in the Rain*, copyright © 1957 by Ted Hughes, by permission of Harper & Row, Inc.
"Status Symbol", from Mari Evans, *I Am A Black Woman*, published by Wm. Morrow and Company, 1970, reprinted by permission of the author.

"My Parents Kept Me . . .", from Stephen Spender, *Collected Poems 1928-1953*, by permission of Faber and Faber Ltd.
"The Wolves", from Allen Tate, *Poems*. Copyright 1931, 1932, 1948, Charles Scribner's Sons; renewal copyright © 1959, 1969 Allen Tate. Reprinted by permission of Charles Scribner's Sons.
"The Reason I Write", "As The Mist Leaves No Scar", "Suzanne Wears a Leather Coat", from Leonard Cohen, *Selected Poems*, reprinted by permission of The Canadian Publishers, McClelland and Stewart Limited.

"What I Expected", from Stephen Spender, *Collected Poems*, by permission of Faber and Faber Ltd and Random House Inc., Alfred A. Knopf, Inc.
"Cupid's Grin", reprinted by permission of Grove Press, Inc. Copyright © 1964, 1966, 1968, 1970 by Michael McClure.
"Haiku: Two Famous Japanese", from R. H. Blythe, *Haiku*, Vol. 3, by permission of Hokuseido Press and Hallmark Cards, Inc.
"Outwitted" by Edwin Markham, by permission of Virgil Markham.

"The Bear on the Delhi Road", from Earle Birney, *Selected Poems*, reprinted by permission of The Canadian Publishers, McClelland and Stewart Limited.
"To The Poets of the Seventies" by Robert Conrad, © Robert Conrad 1969. From *Doves For the Seventies*, ed. Peter Robins, Corgi Books, 1969.
"Healing of a Lunatic Boy", from Charles Causley, *Johnny Alleluia*, published by Rupert Hart-Davis.
"I Saw A Man With Poppies" by Michael Johnson, by permission of Transworld Publishers, Ltd.

"Portrait" by S-D. Garneau, tr. by Louis Dudek, by permission of Louis Dudek. "I Have Seen The Robins Fall" by Louis Dudek, by permission of the author.
"On Top of Milan Cathedral", from Ralph Gustafson, *Sift In An Hourglass*, reprinted by permission of The Canadian Publishers, McClelland and Stewart Limited.
"Dead Beat", by David J. Lee, by permission of the author and Transworld Publishers, Ltd.
"Childhood", from Frances Cornford, *Collected Poems*, published by the Cresset Press.

"I'd Like", "Making Sense", "Living Is", from Piet Hein, *Grooks 1*, © 1966, by permission of the author. Grooks 1, 2, and 3 are published in Canada by General Publishing Co., Ltd. (Ontario); in the U.S. by Doubleday & Co. (N.Y.C. 10017).
"A Supermarket in California", copyright © 1956, 1959 by Allen Ginsberg. Reprinted by permission of City Lights Books.
"For Hettie", copyright © 1961 by Leroi Jones. Reprinted by permission of Corinth Books.

"The Secret Heart", from Robert P. Tristram Coffin, *Collected Poems*. Copyright 1935 by The Macmillan Company, renewed 1963 by Margaret Coffin Halvosa.
"Corner", from Ralph Pomeroy, *In The Financial District*, copyright © 1961 by Ralph Pomeroy, by permission of The Macmillan Company.
"End of the Sears' Convention", from Kenneth Fearing, *Afternoon of a Pawnbroker and Other Poems*, copyright 1943 by Kenneth Fearing; renewed, 1970 by Bruce Fearing. Reprinted by permission of Harcourt, Brace, Jovanovich, Inc.

"The Washing of the Infant" by Su Shih, Tr. Robert Kotewall and Norman L. Smith, from A. R. Davis (ed.), *The Penguin Book of Chinese Verse*. Penguin Books Ltd. All rights reserved.
"In Former Days", from John Brough (tr. and ed.), *Poems from the Sanskrit*. Penguin Books Ltd. All rights reserved.
"Norman Morrison", from Adrian Mitchell, *Out Loud*, published by Jonathan Cape Ltd.
"Sillysuit", from Pete Morgan, *A Big Hat or What?*, published by Kevin Press.

"Hockey Players", "Old Alex", "Complaint Received by a Citizen . . .", from Al Purdy, *The Cariboo Horses*, reprinted by permission of The Canadian Publishers, McClelland and Stewart Limited.
"Misunderstanding", from Irving Layton, *Balls for a One Armed Juggler*, reprinted by permission of The Canadian Publishers, McClelland and Stewart Limited.
"Adolescence", "Man With One Small Hand", from P. K. Page, *Cry Ararat!*, reprinted by permission of The Canadian Publishers, McClelland and Stewart Limited.